From Slate

*170 years of Castle Acre School
on Stocks Green*

For Rachel Young

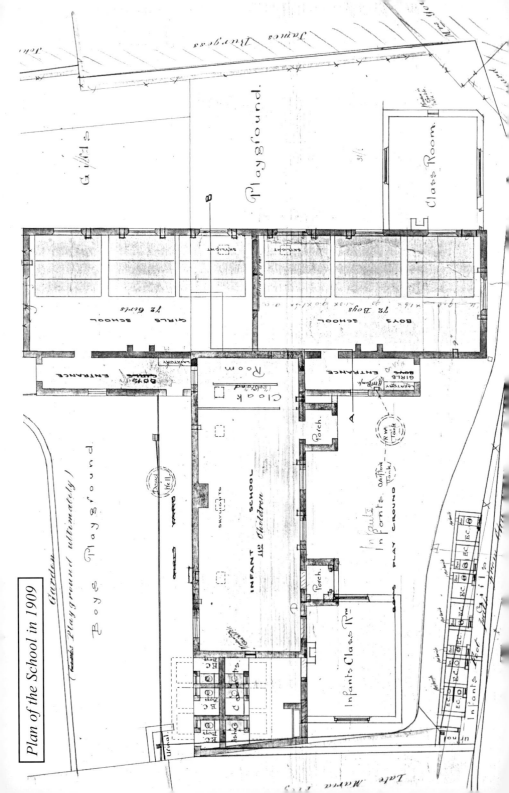

Plan of the School in 1909

From Slates to Screens

*170 years of Castle Acre School
on Stocks Green*

MARY-ANNE GARRY

LARKS PRESS

in association with

BEAGLE PUBLISHING

Published by the Larks Press
Ordnance Farmhouse, Guist Bottom, Dereham NR20 5PF
01328 829207
Larks.Press@btinternet.com
www.booksatlarkspress.co.uk

in association with Beagle Publishing
Fiddlers Green, Castle Acre
King's Lynn, PE32 2BT

Acknowledgements
Rachel Young for generously allowing me to draw on her research
Viscount Coke for allowing access to the Holkham Archives and Christine
Hiskey the archivist there.
The staff at the National Society Archives, Lambeth Palace Library and
the Norfolk Record Office,
Megan Dennis at Gressenhall, Mr Kenneth Kay the Headteacher of Castle Acre
School, Miss Jenny Cooper, Mrs Karen Howman and Mr Derek Thackray.
For supplying photographs and memories: Mrs Janet Boldero,
Mr Russell Boldero, Mrs Rosemary Bell, Mrs Jean Joice, Mrs Queenie Parker,
Mrs Joyce Creed and Mrs Laura Lord.

Front cover drawing by Carole Radley
Back cover: Castle Acre School emblem designed by Joan Matthews
reproduced by kind permission of Mr Kay.

British Library Cataloguing-in-Publication Data
A catalogue record for this book is available
from the British Library.

Contents

The first day of school milk, 1935. The schoolmaster is Mr Crowther

Foreword

This account has been written to mark the move of the Castle Acre School to its new premises in 2009.

The research was initiated by Rachel Young, an authority on schools in Norfolk, who studied the school records in the early 1990s. The research on schools in Castle Acre pre 1870 and all the additional material is mine.

For her research Rachel used the school log-books April 6, 1874–March 18, 1986 with separate log-books for the Infants February 2, 1885–March 31, 1919; a broken run of admission registers April 4, 1874–April 29, 1946; minutes of meetings of the School Managers, account books, and rate books. Rachel wrote that the log-books 1874–1912 'are exceptionally detailed and informative, but the entries for the 1960s are very brief'.

She concluded: 'The comments of the Head teachers and of the H.M.I.s* in the log-books show that this was, especially in the earlier period, often a problem school with low academic standards. The main cause was undoubtedly the poverty of most of the children, especially in the periods when agriculture was deeply depressed viz. 1875–1914 and 1918–1939. Irregular attendance, early leaving, too few staff, too little money, an inadequate and often ill-maintained building, all contributed to poor results at a time when more and more was being demanded of schools – more adult staff, better trained staff, better buildings and equipment, a wider curriculum. But these records also show that determined, able, long-stay teachers could and did effect considerable improvements. Nor was Castle Acre School unique; there were schools in late nineteenth century Norwich, for instance, which were much worse; where the buildings were not just inadequate, but unsafe. There were village schools whose grant was cut and one which lost its grant and shut down.

These records also illustrate the important part played by the H.M.I.s in bringing about improvements – if necessary by threatening to reduce the grant. They appreciated the problems of the staff and were quick to record improvement and, on occasion, reward progress with a higher grant. These records are a valuable source of information about the development of a village school. They are in good condition and should be carefully preserved.'

* H.M.I. stood for Her Majesty's Inspectors; they were replaced by Ofsted in 1992.

FORM 146a (1).

NORFOLK   EDUCATION   COMMITTEE.

LABOUR   CERTIFICATE.

PERMISSION TO LEAVE SCHOOL,

UNDER   BYE-LAW   5 (b).

I Certify that _Elizabeth Bloye_

residing at _Castleacre_

is not less than **THIRTEEN** years of age, having been born on

the _15th_ day of _February_, 189 _6_, as

appears by the Registrar's Certificate [_or the Statutory Declaration_]

now produced to me, and has been shown to the satisfaction

of the Local Education Authority for this district to be

beneficially employed, and has made _350_ attendances after

5 years of age in not more than two Schools during each

year for five years, whether consecutive or not, as shown

by the Certificate furnished by the Principal Teacher of the

Castleacre School.

Dated this _thirtieth_ day of _June_ 190 _9_ .

Secretary to the above-named Committee.

The Child named in this Certificate is exempt from School attendance before the age of 14 years only so long as the Child continues to be beneficially employed to the satisfaction of the Local Education Authority.

2,000—7.08.

8

1. 1712–1838

The earliest record of education in Castle Acre is in 1712 when the Revd Ambrose Pimlowe gave Mrs Elizabeth Smith five shillings and eight pence from the alms money to teach four poor children to read. Mrs Smith continued to receive annual payments, which implies she ran a school, though there are no details as to where this school was, nor what the children were taught; but reading would have been encouraged so they could read the Bible, as well as simple mathematics and writing.

The Cluniac monks who inhabited the Priory from the twelfth to the fifteenth centuries had never been educators and would not have taught the local population, though they were highly skilled themselves in writing and illustrating books. However it is possible the parish priest may have taught some children, using a room in the church; it was the custom to have a schoolroom above the porch.

The payments made to Mrs Smith continued until 1725 when a schoolmaster arrived in the village, though Mrs Smith lived on until May 1733. In her last illness Pimlowe took the sacrament to her privately, that is at her house; his custom of addressing her as Mrs Smith shows she was an educated woman, (not all schoolteachers were) for in a rural village such as Castle Acre the appendage 'Goody' was more common at this date. In Mrs Smith's case the title Mrs was a courtesy one – when Pimlowe entered her burial in the register book he described her as 'single'. No more is known about her as she did not leave a will.

The schoolmaster who arrived in 1725 was Marmaduke Summer-scales, almost certainly a friend of Pimlowe's for like the vicar he came from Lincolnshire. The first time Pimlowe mentions him was to pay him one shilling and sixpence for teaching 'Baily Marrinell's son, the clerk of the parish.' Summerscales was trustworthy and diligent, but he struggled to make a living in Castle Acre. So hard pressed was he that three years later Thomas Coke of Holkham, the landlord, paid him £5 charity money towards teaching 'the poor children to read and write'. Coke did not go as far as endowing a school where the children would have been educated free, though he may have considered doing so.

A few village schools at this date were endowed by local benefactors who left money, usually rent from land in the parish, such as Saham Toney near Watton where the Free School was endowed in 1626 and one in Bawdeswell in 1730. But this was not the case in Castle Acre; here the schoolmaster needed to be self supporting, that is his school was fee-paying.

In 1730, just six months after her husband's death, Summerscales married Elizabeth Whiskerd, a Castle Acre woman who had been twice widowed and was the mother of several children. From her second husband she had inherited a freehold cottage next to the Bailey Gate, 'newly built', a horse and a mule, and assets to the value of £24. Despite this step up in the world, the security of a home, and an advantageous connection to a Castle Acre family, Summerscales still failed to prosper; five years on Pimlowe records giving him a shilling when he set off on his travels to 'try for a School' elsewhere. How he got on we do not know but by 1749 he was back in Castle Acre, probably no better off, for Pimlowe then records buying him two shirts. Summerscales died in the village in 1753 and his widow Elizabeth in 1761.[1]

Meanwhile, as Summerscales set out to seek employment, a schoolmistress Mrs Helen Beales is recorded in Pimlowe's tithe book of 1735. Twice in 1739 Pimlowe gave out six shillings for a quarter's schooling of two poor children by the name of Davey and again three shillings and eight pence for two unnamed poor children. These may have been taught by Mrs Beales or else by Isaac Tolhe who is entered in the parish registers as schoolmaster in 1739 when he and his wife Susan had a daughter baptized. In 1768 a schoolmaster named James Large was buried in the churchyard. Next John Hill is recorded as having been a schoolmaster from 1766 to his death in 1816, from which we can deduce that a schoolmaster was present in the village for most of the eighteenth century and into the nineteenth, teaching any children whose parents could afford the fees. Firm evidence comes some years later, from *White's Directory* of 1836, when 'two academies' are listed, one run by Robert Mayes and the other by John Pratt, who was also the deputy overseer.

Coinciding with the death of John Hill in 1816 was the foundation of a mission whose purpose was to found a Church of England School in every English and Welsh parish throughout the two countries, designed to educate the poor. This was, and is, known as The National Society for Promoting Religious Education. By offering grants to prospective founders, on condition that development was fostered on chosen lines, the Society aimed to fund the building and fitting up of schools and to train teachers. It also aimed to supply reasonably priced religious books for children. The Society became involved with the foundation of the majority of Church of England Schools in England and Wales, which were known simply as National Schools, although as we shall see, affiliation to the Society was not always straightforward. The leading light of this Evangelical mission and the person who initially provided its funds, having made a fortune as a Government contractor during the Napoleonic wars, was Joshua Watson. The Evangelicals of the early nineteenth century were rightly much concerned with the saving of souls, be it converting slaves to Christianity or factory reforms, both of which involved children.

Some parishes were quick off the mark to get themselves a National School; Binham in north Norfolk did so in 1817, though five years later, despite seeking subscriptions from all and sundry, found itself in dire straights.[2] Building and maintaining a school at this period was a struggle, for the countryside was in the throes of an agricultural depression after the French wars and farmers, usually the mainstay of such enterprises, had very little money to spare. Moreover the whole question of educating the poor was open to debate; it was almost more controversial in the nineteenth century than it had been in the eighteenth, with the shadow of the French Revolution still hanging over the land. It was one thing to teach children to read, as Blaikie the Holkham agent acknowledged; he saw the merits of religious instruction, but not of literacy – that is, reading was all very well and good, but imparting the power to write might lead to the production of seditious pamphlets and unrest in the land. His was not an uncommon view. Blaikie was concerned therefore when, in 1822, Thomas William Coke built a new school at Holkham, although this was to be directly under Holkham's control, not the church's nor the National Society's.

However an additional hazard, as Blaikie saw it, was the arrival of the school teachers who would live in the parish and teach at the school. He considered that at all costs 'these people', the new Schoolmaster and Mistress (the man's wife), must be prevented from obtaining a settlement in the parish. To make sure of this he sought legal advice from Mr Deeker of Walsingham: 'The Schoolhouse, School rooms, offices and gardens attached might properly be valued at £10 per an the whole is Mr Coke's property. Suppose Mr Coke places these people in those Schools, rent, tax and rate free, and agrees to give them a certain sum of money weekly on condition of placing a certain number of Poor children under their tuition, at the same time allowing the Master to take other people's at the customary charge for educating children in country Villages and supposing the said Master to occupy the said premises under those engagements for one whole year, would he and his family gain settlements in this parish in consequence of such occupation. If so is there any other method of preventing settlements being made under such circumstances than by certificate from the parish to where the Master

11

might belong. Your answer will much oblige ...' What he feared was that the schoolmaster might become a burden on the parish and consequently eligible for parish relief, costing the local tax-payers money.[3]

The following year an existing (private) school in Weasenham run by Mrs Sharpe and her daughters proposed a Master should teach two evenings a week: 'such Boys and Girls as are obliged to earn in the day ... reading, writing and arithmetic'. After a long day in the fields or working at home it would be interesting to know how these children managed. On a third evening, girls selected from the most 'deserving' families, would be taught sewing and knitting by Miss Sharpe. Coke agreed to pay £10 a year towards this enterprise with the proviso already mentioned, that the Master should not make a settlement and the school make no demand on the parish. In a letter to Miss Sharpe on this business Blaikie cannot help adding how he personally considers it desirable to teach the children to read the Bible, but not writing or arithmetic. As to religious instruction, he said surely that is the business of the Weasenham vicar, the Revd Campbell. All the same he sent his own 'mite' of £1 a year.[4]

With this lack of encouragement and the general economic climate there was very little chance of Castle Acre getting a purpose built school, especially as there was no resident vicar to promote the case. There had not been a vicar resident in Castle Acre since 1796 and this situation lasted for forty-two years until 1838. The Revd Tickell had preferred to live at Wells-next-the-Sea and seldom visited, leaving the day to day work of the parish to curates, of whom William Gibbs was the longest serving. Gibbs was in Castle Acre for fifteen years from 1815 to 1830, but at the end of this time left under a cloud. Accused by the Bishop of being an idle fellow and failing to fulfil his parochial duties, he was punished (not too strong a word) by being 'reduced' to the curacies of Lexham and Newton where: 'the number being committed to his care being small, and consequently his example less extensively dangerous...' Gibbs had been at Castle Acre during a time of great change, especially during the 1820s when the population increased far faster than it did in other parishes; and the newcomers were largely unemployed labourers seeking work, in the main families with young children.[5]

When Gibbs was moved on (to Newton), his successor the Revd Robert Jackson, primed and fresh to the challenge, took on board all that was lacking in the parish. Arriving in December 1830 he wrote to his patron and premier landowner in the parish, Thomas William Coke of Holkham, outlining his intention of setting up a Sunday School 'on the

National Plan' to be held in the church. Coke approved of this and made a contribution towards it, as did the Holkham agent Mr Blaikie, with the usual provisos. Shortly afterwards Jackson claimed to have an attendance of between 100 and 120 children, more, he wrote, than would fit in the schoolroom at the church, which housed only fifty. This was success indeed. With the permission of Holkham, Jackson purchased a stove and, placing it in the chancel of the church, accommodated the surplus children there. One of Jackson's motives was the increasing competition from Sunday Schools run by non-conformists in the village. By 1831 there were Wesleyans and Baptists, though the Methodists were not to build their chapel in Bailey Street for another seven years.[6]

2. 1839–1870

When in 1836 the Revd John Hague Bloom, a Wells man, was appointed vicar of Castle Acre, he had every intention of living in the village. But the old vicarage to the south of the church was a ruin and would need to be built anew. For the first eighteen months, until it was agreed that Bloom and his family should live at The Grove and not in a new vicarage, they lodged in Swaffham, a distance of some four miles from the village. With Castle Acre's population still expanding (it had doubled since 1800) it did not take him long to see how badly a parochial school was needed, which, he estimated, would need to accommodate at least two hundred children. By 1838 the effects of the Poor Law Amendment Act of 1834 were beginning to be felt, and, encouraged by the fact that the Earl of Leicester (Thomas William Coke was created earl in 1837) had recently contributed towards several new schools on the Holkham estate, Bloom proposed Castle Acre should have one too. The 1834 Act took a fresh approach to the relief of poverty; its aim was to end the dependency culture of parish relief by promoting self-reliance and here education would play its part. From this date assistance was provided by 'His Majesty's Treasury' i.e. the Government, from whom it was possible to obtain grants towards the building and running of schools. Bloom must have heard of the new school at West Bilney, built in 1833 with the combined 'gifts' from the Treasury and the National Society. There was no reason to believe that funds would not be forthcoming from both these sources for a school at Castle Acre.

The next task was to choose a site; a small piece of ground belonging to Holkham in the centre of the village appeared the most 'eligible' and in July 1839 the Holkham agent rode over to view it. Blaikie had retired by this time and his successor was his long time assistant William Baker. In 1839 the piece of land in question was part of the farm that went with the Ostrich pub and was being used by the landlord Mr Rump to grow a crop of potatoes. Nevertheless Baker agreed with Bloom that the spot was well suited and on his return to Holkham wrote to the Earl, who was in London, and soon all was agreed. Mr Rump was to be compensated for the loss of his potatoes and the Earl would give £10 towards the building. Bloom received the authority to go ahead. The land in question is where the school now stands on Stocks Green.[7]

Bloom forged ahead forming a School Committee whose first resolution was to make the Earl sole trustee, as he had agreed to provide the land. The Committee members were exceedingly grateful for the 'liberal grant of a Building Site' and the Earl's 'liberal Countenance and Support.' But despite having a piece of land on which to build the school and £10 in the bank, this was hardly enough – further funds were needed, rather more than might be forthcoming from London. Bloom drew up a subscription list of those who might like to contribute and this included the Bishop of Norwich (a friend of the Earl's and anxious to see almost anything done to improve morale in Castle Acre, remembering the disastrous years under Gibbs), Daniel Gurney (a banker) and Andrew Fountaine of Narford. By this method £150 was promised and the remainder, another £30, should be provided by grants from the Treasury and the National Society, or so Bloom hoped. Confident that they would have all the money in due course, Bloom wasted no time. In August he wrote to Holkham to say the Committee had adopted a 'neat and Substantial plan of semi-Gothic Building Comprising two School Rooms' – each able to contain a hundred children and the whole to cost no more than £180. A week later he wrote again saying the Committee had purchased Mr Rump's potato crop, and that the building of the school had begun – it would be completed in the course of the autumn.[8] The land allocated was just half of the land under cultivation, i.e. only half of the present site.

The plan of the school, chosen by Bloom and the School Board, has not survived, though in his letter of August 19, 1839, which accompanied the application form asking to be united to the National Society, Bloom went into some detail as to the school's dimensions. He began with an account of the existing Sunday Schools in the village, counting both

14

Church and Chapel, which were he claimed, attended by a total of 94 boys and 138 girls. The Church of England had 59 boys and 88 girls, the Wesleyan Methodists 15 boys and 20 girls, and the Baptists 20 boys and 30 girls. The new parochial school was intended to admit 80 boys and 80 girls; the children would be separated by gender but not by age, as was the accepted method. This division was not so much for any impropriety but that boys needed to be taught skills unsuited to girls and vice versa. For instance boys were taught drawing so that they might become draughtsmen or clerks capable of making careful entries into ledgers, girls sewing and housecraft. The demarcation was marked by separate entrances into the school; each had their own porch, the boys on the right hand side and the girls on the left. Bloom must have considered the provision of a third schoolroom for the youngest ones, for he wrote the word Infants, but then crossed it out. There was not to be a separate Infants' classroom until the 1870s. The Boys' Room was to measure thirty-one foot by nine and to be ten foot high, the Girls' twenty-four by nine making an area of about six square foot per child. The building to be constructed out of brick, Baltic timber, Portland stone and slate. He says the children, or rather their parents, will be charged three half pence per child per week. The cost of a Master, Mistress, books etc. will be not less than £50 per annum. He also hoped to put up a gallery in the church for the children when they attended there. The National Society application was signed by Hogg the rector of South Acre, Watson vicar at Newton, Henry Floyd a grocer with a shop on Stocks Green and by Bloom himself.[9]

Bloom had already written to the National Society the previous month setting out his reasons for approaching them, addressing his letter to the Revd Wigram, the Society's secretary. In this he referred to an earlier communication still, to which he had also had no answer. He had told them that the new school would serve the combined parishes of South Acre and Newton as well as that of Castle Acre, home to a total of near 2,000 souls. A slight exaggeration, but no matter. He emphasised the extent of the parish and the poverty of its inhabitants. He wrote how at present Castle Acre has 'nothing that can properly be called a School save a miserable substitute in the shape of a mis-named Day School most inefficiently conducted, with thirty or forty children of both sexes at an exorbitant weekly payment per head.' On the other hand he continued he had a large Sunday School and it was sorely needed, for 'the demoralization and extreme ignorance among the labouring classes is truly deplorable', and not only that but 'pitiful and painful'. In the greater parish, of six or seven thousand acres, he said there were seven occupiers (farmers) of whom only five were desirous of establishing a school. Two declined for mixed reasons. He ended by saying again: 'the poverty existing here is extreme'.[10]

The school was duly built, single storey facing south and north, with a plaque set into the brick work on the south side with the words National School carved on it. There was no provision for a playground as this was considered unnecessary – outside activities were reserved for occasional treats. There was an entrance to the school from Stocks Green and an 'office'. It was finished by October 1839 and the cost was rather more than had originally been anticipated, £247.16s. 9d. The Bishop of Norwich sent £50, the Treasury grant matched the amount raised by subscriptions and collections, £72.13s. 9d, the Swaffham Local Board gave £25, last minute donations and collections raised another £12.16s.0d. It was hoped that the National Society would send £15. The remainder of the land, to the east, some seventeen perches, continued to be let to Mr Rump and worked as a garden. Bloom wrote to the National Society twice in October telling them the school was ready to be opened, and that the cost of the rooms had come to £190, with fittings, entrance gates, fencing and sundries adding another £57.16s. 9d. He said he had heard nothing from them since August. They had still not officially accepted the Castle Acre School within their fold.[11]

Although it was in theory a National School, as the plaque proclaimed, this did not mean it was free for the pupils who attended it and nor was school attendance compulsory. The running costs would need to be met by further subscriptions and donations from local people, school pence from the pupils, and, it was to hoped, grants from the National Society, which itself was now financed by subscribers. As there were actually *two* private 'academies' in the village, not one as Bloom said, the school got off to a poor start as these continued to be attended by village children. In the first year approximately twenty-five children transferred from one of the Dame schools and slightly fewer from the other. A Dame school was still operating in the late 1880s.

By 1842 the parochial school was in financial difficulties and Bloom was once more appealing for funds. In mid-November 1843 he wrote to the Earl and Countess of Leicester asking if they would consider subscribing on an annual basis – he records that at present the school was closed and not likely to open again before January 6. The answer came that the Earl would send £5 every year and the Countess £2. John Hudson, the tenant farmer at the Lodge Farm, took up the cudgel on Bloom's behalf in the 1840s. Writing to the National Society, he informed them that he had been appointed as Treasurer of the school's building fund and that the promised funds had never been forthcoming. He himself had lent the amount needed at the time the school opened, but now threatened them with no longer subscribing if he was not paid back. It is possible that the Society hoped that Holkham would cover the whole cost.

Nor did Bloom give up. He wrote to the Society in February 1853 informing them that the school was in real danger of closing. He appealed to them: 'it is only the last extremity', he reminded them that the school had opened in debt and nothing had been donated by the Society. Finally they responded and in March 1853 he wrote to thank them for the welcome grant of £12.16s.0d., the amount raised by the last minute donations and collections raised back in 1839, and still short of the amount required. Bloom told them how 'a private individual provided £27.2s.0d. so the school had opened on time', i.e. no thanks to them. Now, fourteen years on, it had lost some of its subscribers; two of the vicars were dead, Hogg and Watson. Hogg's successor was the Revd Fountaine, a brother of Mr Fountaine of Narford, and Bloom himself now had Newton with Castle Acre. Several more supporters of the school had 'been carried away by death' and the school was struggling.[12]

Poor attendance was the major reason for the school failing. In 1851 there were 282 children of school age (3–12 years) in Castle Acre; of these only 109 went to school, and several of these to the two private schools so scathingly dismissed by Bloom. Tradition has it these schools were little better than crèches where mothers who went out to work left their children, and this is borne out by later entries in the log-books when, on many occasions, 'new scholars' aged seven or eight years old arrived at the school with no knowledge of letters or figures. In South Acre, of the nineteen school-aged children who lived there, just seven are entered as scholars in the 1851 census, though eight others were being educated at home. Not one child came from Newton, where twenty children of school age lived. The two main farmers there openly recorded how between them they employed eighteen boys and girls to work in the fields. These were presumably the two farmers Bloom had noted as having 'mixed reasons' for not supporting a school. At this date Castle Acre School, built to accommodate 200 children, probably had no more than half that number on the roll. The vicar put the poor attendance down to the 'baneful tendencies' of the gang system which predominated in the village at this era.[13] They were certainly part of the reason. The 1861 census records the numbers of women and children engaged in gangs or 'field work'; here it is shown that the youngest child was seven but most were nine or over. It was not considered wrong for a farmer to employ women and children; in fact it was sometimes regarded as a charitable act, but a sad way to spend a childhood. The children worked alongside their mothers and/or older siblings; 40 Castle Acre children aged from seven to twelve (the school leaving age) worked for the gangs in 1861 as did a further 40 aged between thirteen and fifteen. Nor was gang work the only work done by school-aged children; crow-scaring, and watching animals on roadside verges or on the common were other employments.

The first Head of the new school may have been Samuel Rose, his name appears in the parish registers when his son Thomas was baptized in 1841, and he appears in the census that year aged twenty-five. Samuel was the son of Samuel Rose a harness maker from East Dereham. James Lift is also entered as a schoolmaster in 1841; he and his wife Catherine were both fifty years old that year. In 1845 Josiah Berry appears as National schoolmaster and two years later twenty-two-year-old Thomas Bradfield, with his eighteen-year-old wife Elizabeth as schoolmistress. The 1851 census records that Bradfield was born in Bawdeswell and Elizabeth in Beeston; during their time in Castle Acre they had four children born here. This couple may well have taught at the school; it was the conventional and convenient method – the Master to teach the boys and his wife the girls – but the birth of so many of their own in just five years makes this doubtful. Two other schoolmistresses appear in 1851: Sophia Hill a widow of sixty-nine (first listed in 1841) and a married woman Honor Sculpher aged fifty-six, both born in Castle Acre. Three years later in 1854 there had been another change, *White's Directory* records James Raven at the National School and James Statute.

It was a hard task for any teacher coming to Castle Acre; the general attendance was not only low but erratic, especially as the children grew older, and it grew even harder in the 1860s, when the Government grants depended on attendance and the number of children who passed the yearly examination.

Just two schoolmistresses are listed in the 1861 census: Jane Floyd aged forty-one who lived with her sister described as a stationer and their ten-year-old nephew, William, on Stocks Green, and Anne Thompson from West Bradenham who lived on her own in the Newton Road. Anne Thompson is not recorded in 1871 but she is in 1881, still teaching and living in Bailey Street; by then she was sixty-five. Similarly Robert Mayes and his wife, both schoolteachers, appear in *White's Directory* of 1854, but not in 1861 only to reappear in 1871.

Two governesses are listed in 1871; one worked at Manor Farm teaching the children of Thomas More Hudson, the other was Emma Whiskerd aged nineteen. Emma was a member of an old established Castle Acre family.

Little more is known of the school until the Education Act of 1870, other than the building of a low wall on one side of the school yard. The Revd Bloom wrote to Holkham saying this was much needed and as the castle ditches were full of falling stones, he would like permission to use these to build it: 'About twenty tumbrel loads probably, the quantity falling [into the ditches] is considerable...' In 1848 he wrote to announce the discovery of an ancient well in the school yard 'in a perfect state of repair.' Since the land had only ever been used for cultivation 'under the plough and spade' before the school was built, it was thrilling to find such a relic of ages past. Bloom suggested the Ostrich Inn, which had neither a pump nor a well of its own, might like to use this one, but Holkham replied with firm directions to fill it in.[14]

The school had been registered with the National Society, who had funded it to the extent of £12.16s.0d. and from now on the School Board and later the School Committee believed it to be a National school. In 1871 twenty-nine year old Joseph Peak was the National schoolmaster; born in Wisbech he ran the school with his wife Mary, aged thirty-three, as schoolmistress. The Peaks were one of ten households living at 'Leicester Square', described as adjoining the Newton and Rougham Roads.

3. 1870–1902

The Education Act of 1870 brought about profound changes. The main aim was to create school places for all children from five to thirteen years who otherwise would not have gone to school, i.e. the working class children. Even then education could not be made compulsory; this would have been impossible as there were not enough schools. The National Schools, supported by Voluntary contributions, became known as Voluntary Schools – they were to offer places to all within walking distance. As a consequence of this, Castle Acre had to consider accepting children from West Lexham, though in the end it was deemed too far for the thirteen youngest ones to travel each day. The ratepayers would be expected to contribute to the Castle Acre School in respect of sixteen older ones, who in the event preferred to follow their brothers and sisters to East Lexham. Over the next few years the West Lexham School dwindled to only five children and was finally closed in 1883: '...really there is no one who takes any interest in the school but the curate, the Rector is abroad'.[15] This pleased the Holkham agent as the school could now be let as a house and bring in rent.

In order to accommodate more children the school at Castle Acre needed to expand; it was agreed to build more classrooms, but there was a time limit for this. In order to comply with the conditions set out by the 1870 Act all building work was to be completed with eighteen months of the Act becoming law, putting considerable pressure on the School Committee. A further proviso of the Act was that all records of the school should, in future, be entered in log-books, and in this Castle Acre is fortunate – detailed log-books were kept, with the earliest ones from 1874–1912 being exceptionally detailed and informative.

Administration changes were also demanded: the rate payers were to replace the old School Committee with a School Board and then levy a compulsory school rate to staff, maintain and expand the school. Six years later in 1876 another Education Act made school attendance compulsory unless parents could prove adequate education was provided at home. Free education for all did not arrive until 1891; meanwhile parents had to pay 'School Pence' towards the education of their children, two pence a week for the first child, one and a half for the second and a penny each for other children. This could be quite a burden for a large, poor family at a time when a Norfolk farm worker was doing well if he earned ten shillings a week and the children, if at school, were not able to earn, at any rate in school hours. In May 1889 the log-book records several Infants were away 'for want of school money' and the Infant Mistress noted that their attendance improved when the School Pence no longer had to be paid after 1891. With compulsory attendance a problem arose – could the Head exclude a child whose parents did not pay? The answer eventually given was 'yes' but the Managers must then take the parents to court. For those who could afford it home education, i.e. employing a governess, was an alternative; a governess could be had for the same salary as that paid to a schoolmistress, in the region of £50 a year.

Although Bloom was still alive in 1870 (he had another three years of life ahead of him) correspondence between Holkham and the School Board was assigned to Thomas Moore Hudson of the Manor Farm in his capacity as School Correspondent.

With the need to extend the school by building more classrooms the Board observed that the plot of land upon which the school stood was very small and Hudson proposed that an entirely new school should be built on a green field site called Home Close adjoining his premises. This was rejected by his landlord, the Earl of Leicester, who nevertheless agreed to contribute the major share of the building works £143.3s.1d. More land was needed if the school was to be extended, but by December 1872 nothing had happened, though some moves had been made to convey the school and its site to six trustees. The Holkham agent at this period, Samuel Shellabear, was clearly no more in favour of educating the masses than Blaikie had been; he hoped it would be enough to enlarge the present schoolroom and add just one other. The Board however was in favour of three classrooms and three teachers, however much Shellabear protested, arguing that the expense incurred to provide this would be an intolerable charge upon the parish. The population of Castle Acre was now decreasing from its peak in the 1850s, and the school planned to accommodate just 266 children. Pressure mounted to get the building work done as time was running out; not all the trustees had been appointed, both the lawyers and the agent Shellabear were still unsure about the exact legality of the conveyance and the Education Department 'could offer no advice.'

The original schoolroom, its office and entrance, had only taken up twenty-four and a half perches of the forty-one perch plot once cultivated by Mr Rump. The remaining seventeen and a half were still let as a garden to a Mr Manning, who was now persuaded that his well cared-for plot was needed 'to build an addition to the school… you said you would not stand in the way, and I trust you will not do so…' But Manning had a lease for his garden which did not expire until 1875, and it took over a year to sort this matter out.[16]

Bloom died in April 1873; in August a new vicar the Revd Daniel Collyer had been selected but not yet inducted. Since he was to be the chief trustee of the school it was awkward – he was not expected to arrive in the village until October and then only with the promise of a new vicarage being built. Bloom's widow and her family continued at The Grove and there was, apparently, nowhere else suitable. However, the conveyance, containing various conditions, was finally signed that month: the Earl of Leicester to the Revd Daniel Collyer and others. The others were Robert Leeds the tenant at the Wicken Farm, Thomas Moore Hudson of the Manor Farm, Joshua Love the village surgeon, Thomas Matthews a farmer from Newton and the Revd John Fountaine rector of South Acre.[17] Conditions were set out: when vacancies arose they were to be filled by election and the electors would be all those who subscribed

21

ten shillings a year to the School. The Managers/Trustees must live in or near the three parishes and also subscribe ten shillings a year; there must always be one Manager from Newton and one from Castle Acre. Further, as it was believed to be a National School, under the Society's rules the Managers had to be members of the Church of England. Another school on the Holkham estate at Wighton had a Dissenter on the Board which meant changing its status to a British School, a type which would in time become non-denominational.

South Acre and Newton had been amalgamated for the purposes of education since the school was built in 1839. However the Education Act of 1870 demanded that printed notices to confirm this should be put up on the church doors of South Acre and Newton and a final notice to the same effect put in the newspapers. After the appearance of these notices in December 1872 the Board had just six months to complete the new wing.[18]

Tenders for the work were advertised; any builder interested was invited to inspect the plans and specifications at the Ostrich Inn over a period of two and half weeks. The Managers, as the School Board was now called, pointed out that they would not bind themselves to the lowest tender. The building materials would be provided by Holkham, for as Shellabear wrote to Hudson, 'the carting will not be heavy amongst so many...'; waggons from each of the three parishes would collect what was needed. The walls were to be built with stones collected locally and to contain some red brick which could be purchased from Mr Banner in Castle Acre. Banner, the clerk of the works at Holkham, lived in Castle Acre. A Mr Curtis put in a tender for £438 and this seems to have been the one accepted. Government grants were awarded for each extra child expected to attend the school and Shellabear calculated that at £2.10s.0d. per child they would have more than enough, although to buy a cottage for the Master or Mistress would cost a further £120 to £150. Now that they had agreed on three classrooms it was necessary to engage a Certificated Mistress to teach the Infants, an additional expense and it would not be possible to engage one for less than £50 a year. The Revd Fountaine gave £30 towards building the new classrooms and Holkham, as already mentioned, made up the difference of £143.13s.1d.

Despite references to plans drawn and re-drawn, none has survived; most likely they were given to the builder who, once the job was completed, saw no reason to preserve them. The only reference is that a cloakroom served 72 children and Shellabear's recommendation that the ventilation should be by skylights, which he claimed were more efficient, as well as more economical than dormer windows.[17] Skylights are marked on a later plan and were probably taken out when the chimneys were dismantled in the latter half of the twentieth century. The new classrooms were at right angles to the old, running north-south rather than east-west and on each gable end is the date 1873.

The running of the school was to be financed by a Government grant on the payment by results system (targets), that is to say the amount depended on the report of His Majesty's Inspectors who would come to the school once a year. The Inspectors were employed by, and responsible to, a Committee of the Privy Council. This grant was the major source of income and in 1878 was £131. Occasional subscriptions helped, plus a voluntary rate of a penny in the pound for taxpayers. The schoolrooms were also available for hire outside school hours. After the civil Parish Council was formed in 1894 they met in one of the schoolrooms and paid rent for the use of the room, for coal fires and for lights.

When the school was finally re-opened on April 6, 1874 with Mr Smith as Headmaster, it was organized as three separate Schools viz: Boys', Girls' and Infants', each under an adult teacher, but all in the same building. The age range was three to seven for infants and seven to thirteen for older boys and girls. Some children were admitted before they were three, (Sarah Ann Birch was just two and a half when she first entered in September 1874) and very few stayed on after they were thirteen. In 1874 and 1875, before school attendance became compulsory, forty boys left the school to go to work. At this time it was illegal to employ a child under eight in farm work but the youngest of these was six; most were eight or nine. One of them, aged ten, was withdrawn to work for the farmer at Newton, Matthews, one of the school's trustees and Managers. There were eventually about seventy boys in school, but the numbers fluctuated wildly with boys continually being admitted, leaving and sometimes re-admitted.

Mr Smith stayed at the school just over a year, leaving in June 1875. During his term of office and over the following two years up to and including 1877, the new schoolrooms were used for church services; for as soon as they were ready, being the largest indoor space available in the village, work began on the 'restoration' of the church, placing it out of commission. Smith recorded how on Ascension Day, May 6, 'there was a Holiday today, the school being required for Divine Service.' At the church the old schoolroom disappeared, memorials were re-located, a new tiled floor put down as well as structural work, in part paid for by Holkham, with a donation of £25 towards new seating. In 1876 and 1877 the schoolrooms were required for Ash Wednesday services, Good Friday and Harvest thanksgivings. Whitsun fell in the customary week's holiday when the school was closed and a spring clean was taking place. Presumably the school was also used on Sundays. It was within the remit of the new vicar the Revd Daniel Collyer to organise this and on occasions he requested the school to close for other purposes, such as a Sunday School treat in July 1878. Collyer was a frequent visitor to the school during these first years, very much the critical friend, but in the first year, on more than one occasion, rather too outspoken; Smith recorded how he and Mrs Collyer: 'again found fault with the discipline saying *before the whole of the children* that he "never saw such a school".'[My italics] Collyer was at the outset of his ministry and dealing with the church refurbishment, the building of a new vicarage and the school taxed him. He was disheartened by the general state of the village where his duties involved visiting parents to enquire why their children had not attended school, occasionally taking charge of the school when the Head was absent, and when an incoming head teacher told him there were not enough books in the school for home work, promising to buy some out of his own pocket. He and Mrs Collyer also provided the prizes given out at Christmas.

Smith's successor, Mr Hambling, who took up his duties in June 1875, reorganized the structure of the school; the three 'Schools' were now amalgamated under the new Headmaster and his wife; she taught the Infants. In 1877, however, under pressure from the H.M.I. and with the approval of the Head, whose wife had retired ill, the Infants became a separate 'School'. From then on the Infants sometimes formed a School (though in the same building) with their own head teachers, registers and log-books, and sometimes were part of the main school under the Headmaster. This can make the documents difficult to interpret, the senior part of the school, with pupils of seven and upwards, is usually referred to as the Mixed School. After 1876, when compulsory attendance was introduced with the idea that education should be open to all children whatever their circumstances, many infants continued to be admitted at three years old. An analysis of the 100 children who entered the school in 1889 shows none left before reaching eleven, but only ten stayed to fourteen. Children were still being admitted at three years old in the 1930s.

In 1892 there were 130 infants and 200 pupils in the Senior School. These large numbers caused difficulties; the staff was too small, so was the building.

24

There were particular difficulties for the Infant Mistresses with many of the pupils so very young. Parents were glad to send them to school so that the mother could go out to work. On October 9, 1891 the Infant Mistress wrote: 'I find very great difficulty with the Baby class. Many of them are so very young and troublesome. Nelly Baldwin (a monitress) is not competent to look after them, as she is so young.' Children under five attended very irregularly. By the age of seven infants were expected to move up into the senior classes, but promotion was by attainment and not by age and since attendance was irregular there was always a substantial number of children over seven years old still in the Infants. In December 1892 there were twenty-four infants, out of about 130, who were over seven; the eldest was eight and half. Some of these were disabled, deaf or with poor sight, some would now come under the heading of special needs and some were crippled. In May 1908 the ages of the infants ranged from three to ten. Many entered the senior school but were then sent back; half of the sixty sent up from the Infant room in November 1886 were returned because they did not know the alphabet. Some could count up to ten but no further, none could read, though many, by this time had been in the school four years.

In the Senior School the children were divided into Standards I to VII and were supposed to pass an examination (conducted by an H.M.I., usually in November) before moving on to the next Standard. But many pupils progressed much more slowly. In April 1884 a boy was working in Standard III for the third year. In November 1900, five children were put down into a lower Standard. As most children left before they were fourteen, there were usually very few pupils in Standard VII, as in April 1882 when there were 11 pupils in Standard VI and 5 in Standard V, but 45 in Standard I. Standards were grouped into classes, the number of classes depending on the number of teachers available.

It is not surprising that the pupils did so poorly, considering the conditions in this period of 1870 to 1902. Although the school building had been added to, and the older part refurbished in the early 1870s, it was still inadequate for the purpose, and there were rarely enough adult teachers even by the low standards of the time. The situation was accentuated after schooling became compulsory in 1876. Difficulties in recruitment were marked as Castle Acre suffered from an unfavourable reputation; when the Infant Mistress left in November 1890 the post was offered to four women in succession all of whom declined. The same occurred in the autumn of 1898 when the post of Assistant Mistress in the Senior School was offered to four women: all declined. A fifth then accepted, but failed to appear. Many teachers left after a few months and in one year, 1897, there were four Infant Mistresses, with gaps in between. Relations between the Headmaster and the Infant Mistress were often strained. In 1877, for example, the Head, Mr Hambling, quarrelled with the Infant Mistress because she would not let boys go through her classroom to fetch coal. He told the Managers he would not stay unless she went: she did.

In 1874, when these records begin, and for a long time after, it was assumed that in schools like this, pupils would be taught for most of the time by the young trainee teachers, monitors and pupil teachers, who in turn would be supervised by more experienced staff. In January 1886 in the Senior School, with about a hundred boys and girls, there were two adult teachers, (one a young woman probationer), two monitresses and two pupil teachers, both girls. Until 1902 monitors and pupil teachers were employed by the Managers; they received small payments.

Pupil Teachers had been recognised by the Government since 1846. They had to be at least thirteen years old before they were apprenticed, which could be for three or four years, according to age and attainments. Lena Bilham was apprenticed at thirteen in 1896. But some were older. Willie Leaman, the Head's son, was sixteen. Most had previously been monitors. After 1900 pupil teachers had to be fifteen, but could be probationers at thirteen. They had lessons every day from the Head teacher, or from the Infant Mistress if they were working in her Department. In 1878, for example, the Head taught the pupil teachers every school day from 6.30–7.45 a.m. in summer and from 6.30–8 p.m. in winter. They did homework and sat an exam every year. They occasionally observed an adult teacher take a demonstration lesson. On finishing their apprenticeship, a few won scholarships to a Training College, such as Charles Thrower, Pupil Teacher from 1877, who went to St Martin's College, Chelsea. If successful here, he would become a Certificated Teacher. But one could also take the exams for the certificate while teaching.

Most pupil teachers went straight into teaching. When Agnes Bartle finished her four year apprenticeship on October 31, 1879 she was put in charge of the infants at Castle Acre. She taught in the school till she left to get married in 1888 and the pupils had the day off to attend the wedding. Others took posts in schools elsewhere, for example Florence Pooley who became Assistant Teacher at Wicklewood in 1898, of whom more below.

Monitors could be of any age. They too had lessons and sat exams each year. Some had been in the school for years – for example Mabel Bloy had entered the Infant Department aged two years and ten months. She was on probation as a monitor at thirteen and a half, was a Pupil Teacher a year later, finished her apprenticeship when she was eighteen and a half and taught in the school until she took the scholarship exam for Training College a few months later.

Life was hard for these trainee teachers. They had to teach, prepare lessons, attend classes, do homework and work for exams. This was particularly tough on youngsters who lived in crowded cottages and were expected to help at home. Pupil teachers were only supposed to teach at most twenty-five hours a week, reduced to twenty in 1898, but many taught throughout the day. On occasion they had to cope without any adult support: in February 1894 when the Master, the only adult teacher in the Senior School, was down with the 'flu, the school was run by one Pupil Teacher and two Monitors. Some parents objected to their children being taught by young inexperienced teachers whom they had known since they were born. Both Pupil Teachers and Monitors were at times insulted and even attacked by their pupils or by their parents – in July 1883, a boy was caned by the Head for disobeying and insulting a Monitress. Next day he hit her. Shortly after, his mother, drunk, also attacked her. Subsequently the Managers sued the mother for assault.

It is noticeable how often Pupil Teachers and Monitors were away ill.

The Head frequently complained about these young people, who were very often late and did not prepare their lessons or do their homework. On July 6, 1890 the Head reproved a Pupil Teacher for going out at night with young boys instead of doing her homework; she was aged eighteen and was accused of doing no work in the holidays and not even taking home the notes the Head had prepared for her. She resigned that year. There was indeed a considerable fall-out. One girl being tried out as a Monitress left because of 'hard lessons', another was withdrawn by her parents in February 1893 because she could not do her lessons 'and there was plenty for her to do at home.' Some were dismissed, one boy, a Monitor in 1877, was sacked after he twice failed his exams. He couldn't spell. One girl Pupil Teacher became pregnant; one boy died of TB.

The school building itself hindered successful tuition. All too often in winter the rooms were too cold, for despite the presence of open coal fires, funds for the supply of coal were not forthcoming. In November 1874 the Head wrote: 'Wretchedly poor fires. Boys all ashake with the cold', and in December he recorded: 'Poor fires, no coal'. There were some very long cold winters; in February 1895 there was heavy snow and the Infant Mistress said the cold was so intense that she could not keep the children warm enough to do any real work. In summer, due to poor ventilation, the school was too hot. The cramped, overcrowded conditions contributed to the discomfort. In 1890, 121 infants were accommodated in one room which was divided by a partition (which until 1904 did not reach the roof) into two sections, one twenty foot by sixteen and the other forty-two feet by eighteen. To help increase the space available a gallery had been erected and another was added in 1894; both were removed in 1905. In 1895 the H.M.I. wrote that 'the Infants cannot properly be taught in so crowded a school'. The senior children were also accommodated in one large room also divided into two by a partition. A further classroom was added in 1899 to hold thirty-two pupils, but by April 1908 there were forty-eight children in it.

In winter the schoolrooms were frequently too dark; there was no artificial lighting for many years and on foggy days and winter afternoons it was often impossible to draw, sew or even read. January 9, 1905 the Head recorded that, 'At ten to three it came over so dark that drawing and sewing were impractical'. The pupils chanted tables and recited poems when it was too dark to do anything else.

The décor was generally dingy with few if any pictures or charts on the walls, the lavatories were inadequate and insanitary. Pails were used, although the little boys were expected to urinate into an open gulley only a few yards from the classroom door. There was no running water.

The Infants had no desks until 1889, and the seniors only thirty-six; although these were long desks, seating two or three pupils, they were still not enough to accommodate all the children. The seats had no backs and the desks were of different heights and slopes 'some almost big enough for a six foot man'. The Infants used unframed slates; larger framed slates were used in the Senior School until banned by the H.M.I. in 1903. In that year an inventory listed thirty-one desks containing 120 inkwells in the Senior School, seven blackboards, thirty-three wall maps and a globe, 207 penholders and a selection of copy books, drawing books and squared paper – and 205 slates. The Infants had 132, plus pictures used as teaching aids and a harmonium. The seniors had some pictures to illustrate Object Lessons.

For many years, Head teachers and H.M.I.s alike blamed irregular attendance for low standards in this school. As, under Payment by Results, Government grants depended partly on attendance, this was a great anxiety to the Head teacher. One wrote, 'No one knows the weariness of all this, except those placed in the same position'. He was supposed to enter in the log-book the average attendance each week, noting reasons for any low attendance. Even after attendance became compulsory from 1876 it continued very irregular for years, he recorded on July 6, 1906 how a boy of eight, still in the Infants, had not attended once that year. In 1876 regular attendance became the responsibility of the local Attendance Committee and the Attendance Officer they employed, but the Head teachers at Castle Acre found them often worse than useless. Hambling, the Head in May 1878, wrote, 'Many children who should attend school are about in the streets, some are attending a Dame school. The Attendance Committee are constantly requiring information, filling up forms etc. The result appears to be NIL'. Hambling was very bitter about this Dame school, described as 'twenty-two children in a cottage' run by Anne Thompson in Bailey Street. After much nagging the Attendance Officer did visit it, but said there was nothing he could do – in fact he could have declared it substandard and ordered the children over five to attend a Government-approved School. When an eight-year-old boy was admitted who had previously been at the Dame school he was found to be quite illiterate with no knowledge of letters or figures; Hambling noted he was 'only one case of many…'.

The Attendance Officer, who said Castle Acre was the worst school in his district, did not visit it for months on end. Hambling also complained that the Attendance Committee did not issue summons to delinquent parents who 'can apparently defy the law with impunity'. The first Castle Acre summons recorded in the log-books was sent on February 14, 1879. This was successful – the two boys returned, one immediately, after a magistrate's order. Leaman, Hambling's successor, sent notices to the parents of absentees. On October 16, 1882 he had received 'saucy replies' from two parents. In April 1887 he despatched thirty notes, but received only two replies and just one child reappeared.

October was the month that many families left the village, to be replaced with others, the agricultural year ending at Michaelmas, October 11. New families and new faces added to the school's numbers, the Heads often complained that the Attendance Officer did not hunt out children over five who should be at school. The result of this was that the Infant Mistress had to cope with new entrants, many above the age of five, who were almost or totally illiterate. As promotion throughout the school was by attainment and not age, such pupils were placed in the Babies' class along with children of three. In November 1887 the Infant Mistress wrote that she had that term admitted seven children aged six or over 'who do not know any letters or figures. This happens continuously and makes it impossible for the school to flourish'.

Two main reasons for absence were the weather and illness. Although the school was primarily intended to serve Castle Acre, Newton and South Acre, there were usually a number of pupils from elsewhere, including Westacre, Great Dunham and West Lexham, which involved a long walk. In many winters there was heavy snow, sometimes lasting into April, and heavy rain caused flooding, so that the children could not cross the river. On November 14, 1894 three children fell into the swollen river and the next day the bridges were submerged. In February 1904 the river rose so high that the South Acre children had to be taken home in a farm waggon. Bad weather particularly affected attendance of the infants, who, until they were five, were not obliged to come. Some did not come at all in winter. On a very stormy morning in December 1886 there were only fifteen infants present out of over a hundred. It is noticeable how often pupils were away ill, especially in the period 1874–1902. This was due to poverty and bad housing as well as an overcrowded and insanitary school building. On rainy days the children sat in their wet clothes. 'Wet morning and the children's clothes are offensive'.

There were frequent epidemics of measles, German measles, influenza, whooping cough, chicken pox, mumps and diphtheria. Scarlet fever was endemic for years. There were occasional cases of typhoid and many outbreaks of contagious skin diseases such as ringworm, scabies and impetigo. The local Medical Officer of Health tried to control the epidemics by excluding patients and possible contacts and this of course reduced the attendance. In the summer of 1887 the Infant School was closed for a month because of an epidemic of measles. In the winter many children were away with coughs, colds, and sore throats. Others could not get their boots on because of chilblains. Some of the children were very dirty. In 1895 the Infant Mistress said there were four or five children who were so dirty and smelt so offensive that the teachers would not go near them. She occasionally sent children home to wash.

Meanwhile the Head sometimes suspected that absentees were not really ill. On April 17, 1899 he wrote: 'children at work on the allotments are said to be ill'. Pupils, particularly the older boys, were recorded absent from time to time because they were haymaking, 'horse-leading' in spring, sowing corn (probably 'dropping' for a dibbler) or beating for a shoot at Narford or South Acre. By 1900 so many adult labourers had left the land that there was an actual shortage of labour and boys could easily get casual farm work, even though agriculture was depressed. The Head felt that boys who had been at work in the holidays or in term time were impertinent and insubordinate when they returned to school. An entry for September 18, 1884 reads: 'Most of the big boys have been (and some still are) at field labour where they have an excellent lesson in impertinence and have banded themselves together to be as troublesome as it is possible to be'. Boys usually wanted to leave and go to work, even against parents' wishes.

However the School Managers were sensitive to some seasonal events, and the summer holiday of four or five weeks was timed to coincide with the corn harvest, when whole families worked in the fields and went gleaning afterwards. It was always called the Harvest Holiday. If the harvest began earlier or continued later than expected, then attendance at school slumped. On the day the harvest began in 1891 more than half the senior pupils were absent. Holiday dates were usually altered in such cases with permission from the Managers who were consulted over these matters. Pupils, some very young, were also kept at home to help their parents by bird-scaring or potato picking on the allotments, helping to move house at Michaelmas, gathering blackberries and taking dinner to men working at a distance. Girls, often from the Infants' class, were kept at home to mind the baby while the mother went out cleaning or washing.

Truancy was a further cause of non-attendance; it was mainly the boys who played truant. Occasionally the local policeman was instructed to bring a persistent truant to school; an example was two brothers reported as being 'impossible to handle' after their father left home and their mother was in despair. The vicar asked the policeman to assist in compelling them to attend school. In April 1880 the Head (Hambling) tied together five boys who had played truant as 'flogging was ineffective'. In February 1879 Hambling gave up corporal punishment as an experiment, but took to the cane again in June.

There were a number of more pleasurable reasons why pupils missed their schooling. For those who attended Sunday Schools, and many did, there were the annual treats, generally a half holiday with an outing and a picnic tea. In June 1883 nearly a hundred children were away on a Chapel treat. Before Hunstanton was developed as a popular resort, Snettisham, or even Yarmouth, was a favourite destination. Some of the teachers at the school also taught Sunday School and accompanied the children on these outings. Later Hunstanton became a firm favourite and later still the four or more Sunday Schools combined and just one outing a year was allowed. Half holidays were given for a whole range of reasons, sometimes these were connected with the Church or Chapel, but not always. Many children were taken out by their parents, in school hours, to events at a some considerable distance from Castle Acre, including Agricultural Shows held at Wisbech in 1877 and at Yarmouth in 1890, the Sandringham Flower Show from 1892, the Swaffham Lamb Sales and annual Show, the King's Lynn Mart, shows at Fakenham, the Hunt Steeplechase at East Winch, a circus at Swaffham and another at King's Lynn, as well as sales and harvest suppers – and once a circus in the Ostrich yard in Castle Acre itself. When faced with yet another day of low attendance due to an outside attraction the Head teacher wrote: 'every possible thing occurring in the neighbourhood is given and thought sufficient reason for being absent.' Two annual fairs were held in Castle Acre, the first over two days in May and the second in August; these events could 'compel' a closure of the school 'due to noise', though the August one often fell within the Harvest holiday. The noise complained of was music from the steam organ, for the fairs were held right outside the school premises on Stocks Green.

On February 14 it was a Norfolk custom for children to go round the larger houses in the early morning singing Valentine songs and receiving nuts, oranges and pennies. On February 14, 1889, many infants were recorded being away 'Valentining'. Those who attended all day scrambled for nuts and sweets at the end of afternoon school. The custom gradually died out, but a boy from South Acre was said to have gone Valentining in the dinner hour as late as 1940.

A considerable number of pupils simply arrived too late to be marked on the register, so their attendances did not count. On November 9, 1874, one boy arrived at 3.15 p.m. – afternoon school had begun at 1.45 p.m. On December 1, 1874, only sixteen boys were in the Boys' School at 9 a.m. and forty-six other boys came late. Heads tried various methods to improve punctuality, without much success. On May 16, 1879, Hambling locked the doors at 9.05 a.m. and 2.05 p.m. and refused to admit late-comers. He applied for a more suitable bell to be provided as the hand bell was insufficient for those who lived at a distance. In 1882 Leaman caned all children who came late and kept them in double the time. Reasons given varied. Boys came late because they had been playing marbles; both boys and girls because they were sliding in icy weather. On February 9, 1886, 'Many children late this afternoon, the ponds bearing'. In May 1908 the Head noted that the children from the Wicken were late again: 'They stopped gathering flowers'.

They were not entirely to blame; few of these children can have had a timepiece at home and the church clock was unreliable.

When the children were at school, the curriculum followed was recorded in the log-books in an unusually informative manner, especially during the headship of Robert Leaman (1881–1912) who frequently noted sums and sentences for analysis which he had set for internal exams. On October 10, 1882 for example, for Standard II – whose pupils were supposed to be eight to nine years old – one sum was 300 x 572 divided by 7. Only one child out of twenty-two got this right.

The Payment by Results system, whereby the amount of the Government Grant depended partly on the attendance and partly on the performance of each child in an annual exam in specified subjects, conducted in the school by an H.M.I., lasted until 1898. In order to attempt this exam the school followed a prescribed curriculum and in addition the children, both infants and seniors, were examined each year in religious knowledge by a Diocesan Inspector who was usually very pleased with the results.

The basic exam subjects prescribed by the Government were reading, writing, including handwriting, spelling, and correct written English, and arithmetic, including mental arithmetic. Pupils could also be examined in not more than two additional subjects, chosen from a list. Successful pupils in these subjects earned additional grants. The subjects usually attempted in the school were geography: drawing maps and learning lists of facts such as the capes and bays of England, and grammar: parts of speech, parsing and analysis.

The girls also had to do plain sewing, which was examined but not individually marked.

The pupils were taught singing – secular songs as well as hymns – and learned poetry by heart. For November 25, 1884 the poems selected were:

Standard I	Good Night and Good Morning
Standard II	Lucy Gray
Standard III	The Village Blacksmith
Higher Standards	Extracts from Paradise Lost Book I

During their visits the Inspectors heard the children sing and recite. There was a grant available for class singing.

There was also drawing, particularly for the boys when the girls were sewing. When Hambling was Head he put some pupils in for drawing exams run by the government. In 1876, thirty-one out of forty entrants were successful; this earned the school £3.9s.0d. in extra grant. The aim was neat and accurate representation of the object depicted; still a marketable skill at this date.

In addition there were object lessons, usually on natural history topics, illustrated by objects, pictures and drawings on the blackboard. These were intended to increase the pupils' general knowledge. Objects included the canary, a railway station, a pair of scissors, the wind, a thimble, thunder and frost.

Time-tables, schemes of work, lists of songs and poems to be learnt and topics for object lessons had all to be submitted to the H.M.I.s for their approval. Teachers had virtually no choice in what they taught and any deviation from the usual time-table had to be entered in the log-book, which was later read by the Inspectors.

In the period 1874–1902 there was in the Senior School no physical education, no practical work except sewing, and no systematic teaching of science.

Infants 1885–1898

The separate log-books for this period show that the infants had a fairly varied curriculum. The Inspectors examined the infants but did not test individual children.

By the time they were seven and should have moved into the Senior School, the children were supposed to know the alphabet and be able to read and write simple words; they should be able to count and do simple sums. Many, however, failed to achieve this.

The older infants, both boys and girls, were taught to sew and knit. April 22, 1890 – 'Four of the best sewers were given handkerchiefs to hem as a reward for their progress'. December 16, 1890: the H.M.I. wrote 'the sewing of the Second Class boys is very poor'. The children also did kindergarten handiwork such as paper folding and mat sewing, and some drawing. They learnt to sing on the Tonic Sol-Fa system and had some action songs. Musical drill was introduced in June 1890. They also had object lessons – twenty-four in 1892, mostly flowers, trees, animals and birds, but there was also one on 'writing a letter' and another on the Post Office.

Equipment mentioned includes pictures, charts and kindergarten material such as bricks and beads. October 3, 1890, Peak Frean (manufacturers of biscuits) presented two pictures: 'They have been hung on the school wall and look very bright and cheerful.'

From 1902 onwards there was to be increasing pressure from the L.E.A. as well as from the Inspectors, for more physical education, more practical work and a less academic approach – though this was very slow to materialize. In 1898 sewing for girls was the only practical activity. They made underwear – in 1892 the materials ordered included shirting and red flannel. The garments were sold for school funds. Some girls won prizes for needlework, entering in the annual competition organized by the Freebridge Lynn Society for Encouraging Skilled Labour. In 1902, eight girls won prizes ranging from five shillings to one shilling.

There was no physical education nor any team games in the Senior School in the nineteenth century and even a mid-morning break in the playground was only an occasional treat as on May 2, 1890: 'Being a lovely morning the children were allowed 10.45–11.00 a.m. in the playground, the first time since last Harvest Holiday', that is since the previous September.

Overcrowding, learning by rote, and no opportunity for exercise – no wonder discipline was a problem. Henry Smith, who had charge of the Boys' department of the new school in April 1874, found his pupils difficult and, in the end, impossible to control. This was not surprising, as he had up to seventy boys of mixed age and ability, including four of his own sons, and at most one young monitor to help him. He eventually resigned, after repeated complaints from the parson. He left June 17, 1875, by which time there were often only fourteen or fifteen boys present.

His successors managed to keep control of the reorganised school, with boys and girls being taught together throughout. But there were many discipline problems, especially when school attendance became compulsory from 1876 onwards. This bought pupils into the school some of whom had been at work for years: they did not want to come and their parents did not want them to come either. In the past, teachers had been able to expel disruptive children, but this was now more difficult if the child was of an age when attendance was compulsory and there was no other school they could attend. Occasionally a difficult child was sent home and the parents ordered to see the Head. There were also a number of transient pupils who arrived in the village with their parents either to attend or work at the two fairs held in May and August. One such family, the Wheatleys, is recorded in the census of 1881. Their caravan was in the yard of the Dun Cow (now the Albert Victor), and they consisted of a mother and five children, of whom the youngest three, Charles aged twelve, Sarah six and James aged five, are described as scholars. As late as 1927 children from the fair were admitted for the few days that they stayed in the village and helped to boost the attendance numbers.

Only the Head Teacher (and the Infants Mistress when the Infants was a separate department) were legally entitled to cane pupils. These punishments had to be recorded in the log-book – later there was a special Punishments Book; corporal punishment was hardly ever recorded in the Infants' Department. Just occasionally a parent would ask for a child to be caned. June 30, 1909, the Mistress was asked by the mother to cane a girl for attacking and scratching other children. The Mistress did as asked; the mother then complained.

Difficult pupils were sometimes reported to the Managers who would then contact the parents. Occasionally a boy who was entitled to leave was expelled – e.g. May 31, 1878, such a boy was expelled for 'persistent disobedience and dogged resistance'. He wanted to go to work and was said to be out of control at home, but on the whole behaviour in the Senior School had improved somewhat by the 1890s, with the exception of one Assistant Mistress who could not keep order and was eventually sacked in 1900. The Head complained that in her class there was 'too much banging and confusion … nothing ever seems to get finished or learnt or taught'.

The chief discipline problems recorded were:

Refusal to work: April 15, 1886, a boy who had been at work and then made to come back to school was constantly 'disobedient, inattentive, saucy and as awkward as he can be'. He was caned, afterwards lay on his desk for twenty minutes and refused to do anything; the Head eventually lifted him bodily off his desk.

Lying: February 20, 1888, a boy was caned for telling lies 'in the most foolish, daring and determined way'.

Attacking other pupils: Often by throwing stones at them. The aggressors were usually boys but occasionally girls. April 16, 1880, a girl bit and scratched another girl in the playground. April 17, 1890, the Head recorded 'a feud among some of the lads, fighting and stoning each other'.

Vandalism: Usually breaking the school windows with stones (sometimes also by boys who had left). November 2, 1882, two boys threw the school key into the paddock and broke windows. January 23, 1895, two boys broke into the school on a Sunday afternoon and damaged the harmonium. Boys were still breaking windows in 1983.

Graffiti: March 10, 1874, a boy was caned and later expelled for writing 'indecent words' on a door in the village. November 21, 1888, a boy 'wrote rude words on the school wall'.

Obscene Language: March 1902 a boy whose language was 'fearfully low and filthy' was sent home and the father interviewed.

Theft: There were occasional outbreaks of stealing, usually from teachers, though not as much as one might expect considering the poverty of most of the children. One week in January 1882 a silver brooch and a 'fall' disappeared from a Mistress's hat in the cloakroom; at the same time two pairs of scissors were taken. A fall could be either a veil, lace or feathers, by all accounts some exotic decoration to which the culprit was drawn; two weeks later neither it nor the brooch had been returned.

Talking in class: Impertinence.

Smoking: Very occasionally.

Trouble between teachers and parents was itself a considerable problem in the early years when the staff had a number of confrontations with angry parents. On January 11, 1889, the Head recorded that he was often detained by parents on his way to school; others invaded the school itself, complaining about the way their children were treated. There was also an underlying resentment in the period 1876–1891, that the children were obliged to go to school and the parents obliged to pay for them, while losing the money the children might have earned. Some parents undoubtedly resented the fact that the children were removed from their control for part of the day and were being taught things which the parents did not know and might think unnecessary. Their main complaints were:

Punishments – the child had been kept in. November 1, 1883, a mother came to fetch her boy, who had been kept in to finish his work. She said, 'I want him and I'll have him'. When the Head put her into the passage, she threatened and swore at him. He reported her to the Managers.

May 23, 1879, a father whose boy had been kept in for five minutes sent 'an insulting letter threatening personal violence'. The letter was sent to the Managers, who told the father they would sue him if he did this again.

Punishment – child had been caned. April 4, 1884, a father 'marched into school' demanding, 'what did you thwack my boy for?' and uttering threats. 'I left him raving in the yard'. The boy had been caned for laziness.

Punishment by Pupil Teachers or Monitors (who were not allowed to use corporal punishment). The accusations were always denied by the trainee teachers and sometimes by the child itself. November 21, 1889, a mother, who was constantly coming and taking her boy out of school, hit a girl Pupil Teacher in the street, saying she would not have her boy kept in or caned. March 12, 1886, a mother assaulted a girl Pupil Teacher, saying her son, an infant, had been caned, but the boy said he had not. After much pressure from the Managers, who threatened a summons for assault, the mother apologised.

Child was taught by trainee teachers. April 28, 1876, two parents complained that their children were not always taught by the Head (Hambling). He replied that if they were dissatisfied they could withdraw their children 'and that I had no intention of being dictated to by parents in the way I managed the school'. At this date there were only two adult teachers in the Senior School and over a hundred boys and girls.

One boy's father told him to go home if anyone but the Head taught him. He had been punished for disobeying a monitress, whom he later threatened. July 3, 1883.

School Pence. June 13, 1881, a boy was sent home for three weeks' money which was owing. His mother sent back an 'insulting and saucy letter'. August 7, 1883, a mother 'came in a terrible rage' because her boy had been sent home for the one penny school pence, she said he had been sent with one penny instead of two because there had been a holiday on Bank Holiday Monday. Heads continued to complain of the difficulty of collecting school pence, which were £6 in arrears in the first quarter of 1887. Very occasionally children did not give in the money but spent it themselves, as on July 5, 1887.

Absent Pupils. January 1, 1902, the Head sent a note to a father asking why his daughter was not at school. Father replied, 'You may send your x....x notes as much as you like, I shall only send her when I like'.

As late as December 1937, the Head (Crowther) complained to the Managers of 'repeated visits of irate parents'.

Hambling, the Head from 1875 to 1881, had arrived at the school with high hopes; he came from King's Lynn and was thirty years old. In Castle Acre he lived in a cottage on Stocks Green with his aunt and his wife Lucie, who was to teach the infants, but she resigned in October 1879 due to illness caused 'by overwork and anxiety'. Two months later the Managers proposed cutting Hambling's salary, presumably because his wife was no longer teaching, a row ensued but a compromise was reached. Mrs Hambling became the Sewing Mistress and a new Infant Mistress was engaged. When Hambling eventually resigned it was because, he said, of the H.M.I.'s report. This, received January 28, 1881, said the children had passed fairly well in elementary subjects but were very backward in grammar and geography. The exam results were often disappointing, though the singing and sewing were frequently commended. H.M.I.s and teachers alike complained that the children mumbled, read without expression and did not understand the meaning of the words they read and recited. (This was a common complaint made, among others, by the poet Matthew Arnold, who was an H.M.I.) Staff also complained that the children copied each other's work and counted on their fingers.

Hambling's successor was a Yorkshire man Robert Leaman, he arrived aged forty-one in 1881 and remained until his death in 1912. During Leaman's time the school, especially after 1902, underwent several changes for the better and cannot have been quite the 'worst I have ever seen' as the Attendance Officer had judged it, for the village doctor, Dr Porter, sent his children there and his son Reginald went on to qualify as a doctor in 1912. There were other successes when a child seemingly at a disadvantage shone through. A striking example is Dulcie Gaze who arrived in 1895 aged eight years and eleven months and knew so little that she had to be admitted into the Infants' class with children of five and six. By 1903 she was a Pupil Teacher and qualified as a certificated teacher in 1907 passing her exam with distinction.

4. Admin and the School Building 1902–1949

The new century brought important and far reaching changes to the administration of government supported schools, changing them in effect into semi-state-run institutions. The Education Act of 1902 transferred the control of public education to the Local Authority, in this case, Norfolk County Council. From this date Castle Acre was officially described as a Non-Provided Voluntary School; the Managers continued to believe it was also a National, i.e. Church of England, School, though this issue was not to be resolved for another ten years. Under the new Act the teachers continued to be appointed by the School Managers, but had to be approved by the Education Committee of the Norfolk County Council who paid their salaries, whereas previously the teachers had been paid by the school direct. Until 1902 none of the teachers had written agreements of employment, this was to be rectified. From now on the N.C.C. provided furnishings and equipment for the school, with the Managers occasionally paying for extras, e.g. repairs to the harmonium, or pictures (£4. 2s. 6d in

1921). A check was to be kept on the stock provided for the school in a Stock and Stores book and the Head was further responsible for a Managers' Minutes Book. These articles and many other 'Goods' were supplied by Messrs Jarrolds of Norwich, entered in the newly acquired Stock Book, the delivery forms checked and sent on for payment to W.D. Bushel Esq. at N.C.C. (Norfolk County Council)

Council Inspectors, as well as His Majesty's Inspectors, now visited the school. Where before there had been six Trustees running the school there were now four Managers, called Foundation Managers, of whom one had to be a County Councillor and another a Parish Councillor. Thomas Moore Hudson was still alive in 1902; he was 73, but his position as School Correspondent and Treasurer had been assigned to William Devas Everington, the tenant at Lodge Farm, ten years his junior. The school now had its own headed paper with the words 'Castleacre Non-Provided School no 74' printed above the address. Once again some correspondence between the school and the Holkham agent, now J.M. Wood, survives in the Holkham archives. Help from the N.C.C. did not cover the fabric of the school, for which the Managers were responsible, and this they found increasingly difficult as the building became older, needing more repairs, and at the same time the standards demanded by the County Council rose. The Managers ran into debt, though only for small amounts.

They raised money by levying a voluntary rate each year, as in previous years when Lord Leicester had donated approximately half as much again, about £26. A balance sheet for the year 1887 shows the staff were paid £180, books £20, coals and cleaning £18, repairs £10 and sundries £6 with the local rates raising £55 and an education grant of £143. Costs had risen considerably by 1902 with the staff estimated to cost £350 in wages, books £25, coals and cleaning £15, sundries £2 together with extras making £470 for the year. The education grant was £228, aid grant £40, fee grant £114 and the voluntary or local rates £80. This was never enough; jumble sales and fêtes were organized, the schoolroom was let for meetings at bargain rates. Occasionally the Managers got some help from the Norwich Diocesan Board of Finance; in 1932 this was £5, by 1934 £20 was given from a charity plus a loan of £40. Donations were rare, just four in 1910. When the Managers appealed to the Education Committee for help they were advised to change the status of the School, either to Aided – when the N.C.C. would pay half the maintenance costs – or Controlled, when the N.C.C. would pay the whole costs.

The Managers got very little support from the Castle Acre vicar despite this being, in theory, a Church of England School. After Bloom died in 1873 his successor Revd Daniel Collyer appears to have been something of an invalid. The 1881 census lists a 'sick nurse' living at the vicarage and the log-books of the period record that he was often unwell. He taught religious instruction but not creed or catechism and after his initial involvement all too often his school duties were performed by others, his curate or neighbouring clergymen. Disturbed by the poverty he saw in the village he did, however, set up a fund to finance a soup kitchen. When Collyer retired 'to live abroad' in 1890 the soup kitchen was taken on by others, for the next vicar, the Revd Powell, did very little in the village, to the point of negligence. In 1903 Everington, the School Correspondent, wrote that Powell 'takes no interest whatever in school and never enters it except for meetings…. he has not entered it for twelve years' – that is since the day he was inducted. Even the Holkham agent, J.M.Wood, agreed that: 'The vicar is useless but I do not think it advisable to create a precedent and cut him out.'

The Managers wanted to know if Lord Leicester would undertake the repair of the school building 'or assist in any way' as in the past he had been so supportive and taken such a kindly interest. In a letter to Holkham, Everington refers to his own duty, which was to return the school papers to the Education Department, thus handing the school over to them and he was naturally anxious that the documents should be clear and in good order. The South Acre vicar the Revd Daubeney had wanted Everington to fill in the form saying the school was a church one, but Everington, referring to the deed of August 1873, explained he could not do this. He wrote: 'The deed simply provides an Elementary School and that the Creed and Catechism have to my belief not been taught.' He was correct; the deed stated that the 'said land schoolroom and premises and all the buildings thereon erected or to be erected to be forever hereafter appointed and used as and for a Public Elementary School and School House within the meaning of the Elementary Education Act 1870.' There was no mention of it being a Church of England school. In fact Daubeney had no real say in the matter anyway having been appointed as a School Manager in error, as Wood the agent was quick to point out. The Managers had appointed one Manager too many, in particular '… the [South Acre] parson who seems inclined to be more energetic than some think desirable'. Wood wrote to Lord Leicester to say he intended to be present at the next meeting of the Castle Acre School Managers when 'my presence might check the South Acre parson and save friction.' A representative from the Department of Education also seems to have attended this meeting but Wood smoothed the way and the transition was completed with no further mishaps.[20]

The 1902 Act in effect ended all links the school had with Holkham, once the forms were handed to the N.C.C., though that did not stop Holkham from being a provider. When, a few years later, the school underwent repairs and alterations at a cost of £198, Holkham gave them £65.[21] Everington was reluctant to become one of the new foundation Managers, but he continued for some years as Correspondent and was one of the three Castle Acre trustees, the others being Powell, the vicar, and Mr High, the latter chosen because he was 'comparatively young and a very useful man'.[22] Meanwhile, Everington notes that Hudson had became 'a young man again' on being offered Lower House to live in but he took no future part in running the School.

Everington, who had dreaded the school being turned over as a Provided School which would have given the authorities control over any religious instruction, almost changed his mind two months later in March 1903 when it was rumoured that the playgrounds were to be asphalted 'for drilling children' – the Managers would be asked to pay for the cost of this plus some equipment, dumb-bells and batons, which they all objected to. If this sort of thing were to continue Everington said, writing in confidence to Wood, perhaps after all they might be better 'going over to a Provided School and shirk the responsibility'. Quite why the prospect of drilling the children, who enjoyed few outdoor activities during school hours filled him with such gloom is unknown, unless he foresaw it leading to further expense, or to the children expecting new popular activities such as scouting. (A village child had been baptised Baden Powell Dutchman three years earlier.)

Slowly the standard of living improved; the soup kitchen founded by Collyer in the 1870s and which had been housed since 1890 in a cottage on St James's Green (with the rent paid first by Mrs Hudson and then Mrs Leeds of the Wicken Farm) closed its doors in 1905. Soup kitchens were more usually found in urban settings and its long presence in the village is significant. Between 1901 and 1917 Holkham bought up over fifty cottages in the village and either pulled them down, if deemed uninhabitable as many were, or improved them, often by joining two cottages into one. Fewer cottages were needed as the population declined from its height in the 1850s.[23] Even so, in the winter of 1900 Mrs Everington appealed to Holkham for a donation towards giving out coal to the poor[24] and the insanitary conditions of most dwellings meant that the spread of disease was almost unstoppable, resulting in poor school attendance and worse; it was not unusual for school age children to die of scarlet fever, typhoid, measles or whooping cough. With this in mind it was suggested that the school should undergo improvements to alleviate the overcrowding in the classrooms and improve the general hygiene.

In 1909 plans of proposed alterations were sent for approval to the Board of Education in Whitehall who replied with a (hand-written) list of suggestions. With the exception of recommending a larger window for the Infants' classroom, most had to do with sanitary matters. The Boys' earth closets were too near the [existing] windows of the Infants School, there were not enough closets for the Girls, the urinals must be able to be flushed etc. The plans, for which the contract was signed on September 13 1910, shows the school with three large schoolrooms and two smaller classrooms. This gradual change in school design from large school-rooms holding several classes to a separate room for each class was the trend, though it went no further. In 1935 the H.M.I. complained that the two top classes shared the same room – which in earlier times would have been taken for granted. The main alterations proposed in 1909, and subsequently carried out, were the building of a new classroom to the south-east of the building which would later become the kitchen, a new doorway out of the Infants' playground onto the lane which led to the church, a new window in the gable end of the Infants' classroom, 'improved' loos and fenced playgrounds. The work was carried out by J.F. Impson of Station Road, Swaffham, who sent in a more competitive estimate than did Mr Boddy of Tittleshall. Impson wrote a typewritten estimate on headed paper, he had no telephone in 1910 but had been established as a builder for thirty-five years. By contrast all letters from Holkham continued to be hand-written, as were those from the Board of Education in Whitehall, who did not have headed paper either.

The 1909 plan shows separate cloakrooms for Boys, Girls and Infants; previously the Girls had shared with the Infants. There were no lavatories shown on the conveyance plan of 1873. Those for the Infants were to remain and those for the Boys and Girls to be replaced by new ones in the playground provided with boxes of dry earth, although all were considered to be too close to the school building, which was difficult to avoid given the small area of ground around the school. A purchase of 'sanitary pails' in October 1917 shows that the lavatories were, or were about to become, pail closets. By 1944 a scavenger was being paid by the Rural District Council to empty pails once a week. In October 1949 the

Abbey Augustus Taylor with his parents; he was a pupil at the school from 1910–1914.

Managers complained that this was being done within school hours, but despite this in 1950 the Council was still refusing to allow the scavenger to come more often. The Managers employed a man from 1948 onwards to clear the drains and scrub lavatories and paid him £1 a month.

The 1909 plan shows a rainwater well with a pump in the new girls' cloakroom, but no running water. The following year there are payments for water carting, which suggests this well was empty in a dry summer. In 1928 the H.M.I. complained that 'no arrangements are made for children who bring their midday meal, and for their supply of drinking water, they are dependant on the kindness of neighbours'. The drinking water, later supplied in June 1939, was said by the M.O.H. to be 'unsuitable'. When, however, the school kitchen was constructed in 1945, a well was sunk and a pump fitted. In 1949 the local Education Authority was asked to provide a drinking fountain.

In 1910, as these improvements to the school were going ahead, Everington wrote to the National Society informing them that alterations were taking place and that they would cost £160; he asked for a donation. He believed, as everyone else did in Castle Acre, that the school was affiliated to the Society. The Society however replied in the negative: as far as they were concerned the school had no connection with them and they denied it ever had; they asked the Castle Acre Managers what evidence they had for believing it was a National School. What proof could the school offer? After some head-scratching the Managers came up with three pieces of evidence: the first was it said so in *White's Directory*, and the second was that Bloom had said so in his book on Castle Acre published in 1843. Finally they described the plaque in the south wall of the original schoolroom which, although it had no date, was clearly contemporary with the building and not added later. On it were carved the words National School.

Talbot Baines, the secretary of the National Society, was still not convinced, he doubted it had ever been a Church of England school. The Managers must have sent a copy of the trust deed along with their 'evidence', for he rejected that as well, saying it did not count as proof. For proof he had only to consult the Society's records and read the correspondence Bloom had had with his predecessor, but instead Baines wrote to Canon Fardell of the Norwich Diocesan Association of Schools recording his doubts. Fardell suggested the Castle Acre Managers should submit to the National Society an agreement that in future the school would be a Church of England school. Baines begrudgingly wrote, that, if they did that, then the Society would agree to a provisional grant of £10 towards the school alterations. In May 1911 Fardell instructed the Revd Brereton of Little Massingham, the Diocesan Inspector of Lynn Norfolk Deanery, to visit Castle Acre and make a report, which he did. Brereton said the Infant Mistress Miss Tuck had 100 children to teach with no church funding and that she was in need of 'religious apparatus for religious teaching', suggesting that if the School Managers would agree to spend £2 on this, then the National Society should pay a grant. In mitigation he added that Castle Acre had a large population of *poor* and no resident squire, that the living was a poor one, that the school was the largest in the deanery with 250 on the roll and that there was a great need to keep the children interested in religion. 'Religious apparatus would

Pupils in front of the school (date unknown)

help in this.' The National Society digested and discussed the report and finally agreed that the Committee would 'probably make a grant in this case'. Everington wrote to Baines in July 1911 explaining, much as Bloom had done seventy-two years earlier, that Castle Acre was a purely agricultural parish with very few resources, the alterations to the school were finished, please send the £10 as promised. He wrote again the following month, saying yes please the Managers would be happy to sign the Society's application form and finally the school was taken into the fold of the National Society.[25]

Meanwhile back at the chalk face the small playgrounds on the original site continued in use, that is the Girls' playground to the east of the School building, the Boys' to the north and the Infants' to the south. Given the number of children in the school and the size of the playgrounds there was very little scope for games but an additional playground was later added on the south side of the footpath to the church, on land belonging to the Earl of Leicester, which he subsequently gave to the Managers on March 9, 1914. There were frequent complaints of the poor state of the playgrounds, which remained gravelled, until the Girls' playground was macadamized in October 1934. One of the school yards was tarred in 1924; earlier in 1911 there had been a considerable problem when the roads were tarred, probably for the first time, and children arrived at school 'in very dirty boots making the school floor in a dreadful state'. In October of same year the complaint was of 'very dirty hands through shelling walnuts'.

Company on the way to school in the 1920s
Photo by Viola Farley

Fifteen new desks were requisitioned in July 1913 and eighteen new double desks were supplied in 1924. From 1930 additional equipment was purchased, some of it bought with funds raised by the school itself, such as pictures to hang on the walls. By December 1933 there were twenty-six pictures including 'The Laughing Cavalier' and a coloured picture of the King and Queen. Some of these were bought with the proceeds of jumble sales, some donated, others given by the L.E.A. Jumble sale money also purchased a gramophone and records. A wireless radio was purchased in 1936 and the licence was pasted into the headmaster's pictorial record of the school's activities. The licence was bought from the village post office, at a cost of ten shillings, and in 1939 the H.M.I. said the radio was being made good use of, with pupils listening to the BBC Educational programmes. It lasted until 1957.

An early photo of Castle Acre Post Office

Heating continued to be a problem; at first there were open coal fires, and later, closed stoves were introduced, fuelled by purchases of coal, anthracite and kindling wood. After 1902 the L.E.A. paid for the fuel, but the Managers had to provide the stoves. In 1948 (after a particularly harsh winter) the Managers tried to raise funds to buy five additional stoves, but only made enough for two. The cold winter of 1947/8 must have made the Managers consider alternative means of heating, for a discouraging letter was received from the County Council saying it was highly unlikely they would pay for oil or electricity, as they considered such heating suitable only in emergencies. As late as 1953 the Managers were still complaining that only one classroom could be heated to the temperature required by the regulations.

There are no references to additional lighting until electricity was installed. In October 1936 the L.E.A. said that if the Managers would install electricity, the L.E.A. would pay for the current. 1936 was the year electricity came to the village.

In May 1931 the Correspondent appointed by the Managers wrote to the agent of the Holkham estate asking him to suggest a site for a school garden on which to grow vegetables, which both the H.M.I. and the County Inspector had recommended. The agent said there was a derelict cottage near the school and the Managers could have the site at a nominal rent if they would clear away the bricks, stones etc. It was agreed that some of the boys should carry out this work as the site adjoined the school playground, though this was not to be an 'official' school garden as that would entail too much bureaucratic interference. The boys were used as the Managers could not afford to pay for it to be cleared. When the site was cleared the Holkham estate charged a rent of one shilling a year. The garden was said to be in Pales Green, adjoining the allotments. By 1938 there was a beehive in the garden, the property of the L.E.A.; in January 1942, during World War II, the vicar gave an additional piece of land so that the pupils could grow more food, presumably part of his garden. After the war a disused Anderson shelter was used as a tool shed but was replaced by the L.E.A. in the autumn of 1949 and the shelter sold. The school garden being adjacent to the allotments, there were problems with people crossing the garden to reach their plots, though this explains why the allotments are still known (2009) as School Gardens.

In January 1942 the Managers agreed that L.E.A. should establish a canteen at the school to provide 150 hot dinners. Traditionally, most children who could went home for their midday meal; the timetable allowed them an hour and those who lived too far away brought their dinners with them. The L.E.A. would pay for the building work and equipment and they would pay the canteen staff, but the Managers would have to pay for the food (until 1949). Owing to wartime delays, the order to convert and enlarge a classroom to provide a kitchen, and to sink a well, was not given until May 1945 – more than three years later. Then the kitchen was made by converting and enlarging one of the small classrooms and the canteen was officially opened January 16, 1946 with a 'preliminary rehearsal' the previous day; the first child in a family paid 5d for each meal, the second child 4d, all subsequent children 3d each. When these prices were increased by 1d in March 1950 the number of pupils buying meals dropped. By 1948 plans were being made to supply meals to schools in neighbouring villages and a Canteen Supervisor was appointed. By October 1, 1948, twenty-six children were receiving free meals, but the Managers doubted if some were really entitled to them.

Though the Managers appointed the canteen staff they had little control over them and protested when Miss Cook, appointed Cook/Manager when the canteen opened, was, in October 1947 suddenly transferred to Litcham, but they protested in vain.

By 1949 the school buildings were once more in a state of disrepair and the County Architect said repairs costing £400 were necessary. The Managers began seriously to consider this, though with reluctance. From 1947 onwards there had been a great deal of correspondence about a proposed new school on the water meadows for which plans were drawn up, but the Managers decided they could not possibly fund the maintenance of this new building and eventually applied for Controlled Status in September 1954.

5. Staff and Pupils 1902–1949

From 1902 there was a gradual move towards the employment of more adult teachers. More became available as pupil teachers taught less and eventually disappeared. In 1901 Mr Robert Leaman was the Headmaster and Miss Tuck Head of Infants, assisted by Louisa Lurkins and Rose Reader. Miss Tuck (born in London) lodged in Castle Acre with Henry Taylor, newsagent, in his cottage on Stocks Green; Miss Lurkins (born in Ireland, though a native of Suffolk) lodged in Back Lane with Mr Elijah Whiskerd whose daughter Emma was a Pupil Teacher at the School.[26] Rose Reader lived with her parents in Bailey Street. There were two further Pupil Teachers, Alice Spencer and Emma (otherwise Lena) Bilham, both Castle Acre born and living at home. Alice was eighteen and following in the footsteps of her older sister Ellen; the others were seventeen. Emma Bilham's father was a Methodist Preacher but this seems to have presented no obstacle for the Managers, and indeed Lena, as she was known, was to be a life-long teacher. From 1903 the Pupil Teachers attended the Pupil Teacher Centre in King's Lynn three days a week. In order to get there they took a trap to Swaffham (2s. 6d) and from there the train to Lynn. The travel costs were paid for by the N.C.C.[27] Gradually the time Pupil Teachers spent being trained at Lynn increased, so that by March 1905 the Pupil Teacher in the Infant School was only teaching for seven and three quarter hours a week. In 1915 Dorothy Ruscoe the daughter of the Head became a Pupil Teacher, but after a few months she caught scarlet fever and had to withdraw. That same year the Head was obliged to dismiss another of the Pupil Teachers, who was

50

considered 'unsatisfactory', just two among many set-backs. Several teachers were aware of the constant turnover among the staff, which combined with the intermittent attendance by the pupils, made continuity almost impossible.

'Oh the dreariness of it after the holidays and bad attendance', wrote the Head in 1903.

When the school was closed for reasons of illness (a measles epidemic) as in May 1917, the Norfolk Education Committee in Norwich was informed and they issued instructions for the Castle Acre teachers to 'supply' other schools until their own re-opened. Miss Lurkins was sent to Walpole St Peter, Miss Tuck the Head of Infants to Edingthorpe near North Walsham, Miss Gaze to Brockdish 'at once' and Miss Goodman to Swanton Abbott. Their travel expenses were paid for by the N.E.C and the Managers of the respective schools they arrived at were responsible for finding them lodgings. Mrs Boddy was posted to Winterton, but protested that as her husband 'will join the colours tomorrow, it will be late when I arrive at Hemsby.' Mrs Boddy had begun in the School in 1898 as Lena Bilham a Pupil Teacher, her husband was a builder and was either the same or related to the Mr Boddy of Tittleshall who had sent the more costly estimate for work on the School in 1909. In less than two weeks, on June 4, Castle Acre School re-opened and they all returned. In July 1918 the school closed again for medical reasons and Miss Lurkins was sent to Melton Constable only to receive a telegram on arrival ordering her to Stoke Ferry. Miss Tuck went to Drayton and Mrs Boddy to North Tuddenham. Towards the end of the First World War, in 1918, Mr Ruscoe, the Head, who had been issued with a certificate of exemption from active service, was nevertheless withdrawn from the school in order to help Mr Everington with the harvest. That year the harvest was late and Ruscoe was still working there on September 21. In September 1920 the school was closed once more and again the teachers were dispersed all over Norfolk, this time the Head, Mr Ruscoe, was included and he was directed to Barroway Drove.

These measures, exacerbated by the shortage of teachers during the war, were not always popular – in 1920 Miss Gaze, who had only to go as far as Brisley, reported she had caught a bad cold, Mrs Boddy claimed to have 'flu and Miss Lurkins arthritis. It was all very well in summer when they were given extra allowances if they cycled to the schools, but, as Miss Tuck wrote in February 1921, the bitter weather she endured on the journey she was ordered to take to Kenninghall, resulted in her catching cold herself. She was doubly put out, being a Head of Infants at Castle Acre but was expected only to assist at Kenninghall.

1919 was a particularly unsettling year. It began with the return of Mr Lane who, prior to joining the Royal Flying Corps in 1915, had been an assistant master; but he stayed for just two months before obtaining a post at St Faith's School. In June Miss Tuck reported scarlet fever in the house where 'I go to dinner every day – I do not lodge there'. This may have been the same house where Miss Lurkins lodged, for she had reported scarlet fever in her lodgings. Fortunately no children were involved and the school remained open. It was the responsibility of the Managers to make alternative arrangements for these two women and to obtain certificates for the prevention of carrying infection. Miss Lurkins went to visit her relations in Suffolk during the Harvest holidays but in September was unable to get back to Castle Acre due to a train strike, she remained stranded in Suffolk and was unable to return until October 11. The same happened to Miss Goodman. In their place a Miss Miles from Walpole Highway arrived as a supply teacher, along with Miss Alice Spencer recently returned to Castle Acre to help care for her family. Her father was a blacksmith living on East Green.

Between 1915 and 1930, besides the Head and the four long serving teachers, Miss Tuck, Miss Gaze, Miss Lurkins and Mrs Boddy, twenty-three other teachers were employed at the school for varying lengths of time. Even so Castle Acre was often under-staffed – for instance in 1920 Miss Ruscoe, who since 1915 had taught at Snettisham, Rudham and Lowestoft, applied to Castle Acre where her father was Head, only to resign a year later to marry Mr Elvin (a Castle Acre neighbour). In 1920 both Miss Lurkins and Miss Goodman resigned, but Lurkins was persuaded to remain and in November the following year, when Mrs Boddy was again on maternity leave, was teaching Standards 1, 2 and 3 – sixty-five children. Miss Lurkins eventually left in 1928, after twenty-eight years.[28]

The vexed question of married teachers was often discussed, Mrs Boddy being a case in point. Mrs Boddy applied for maternity leave in 1917: 'I expect my accouchement in the middle of October and in accordance with the Handbook, send word four months before the time', adding that she had enjoyed her recent brief posting to Winterton. Mrs Whiskerd late Pooley offered her services to cover the period when Mrs Boddy was to be confined. Mrs Whiskerd lived in Bailey Street and in her letter accompanying her application form said she had been a Pupil Teacher at Castle Acre under Mr Leaman, as indeed was the case; since when she had taught five years at Wicklewood and four at Beccles. By now she was aged thirty-seven, married but with no children and her husband was about to join the Army. She was taken on for two months, the allotted time allowed for childbirth leave, although Mrs Boddy was away three months on half pay.

The Managers became increasingly reluctant to employ married women as teachers, and in 1919 proposed dispensing with Mrs Boddy on the grounds that the pupil numbers had dropped and that she was pregnant once more. However this did not happen. In 1922, they engaged Mrs Seal from Blackburn who came highly recommended by Miss Maud Atkins, the Head of Swaffham School. Mrs Seal was probably a war widow; she had been in India in 1916 teaching at the Sacred Heart College in Bangalore, and was now alone with a child. What she knew of Castle Acre we cannot know, only that she arrived to take up her post on April 4, 1922 and resigned three weeks later, stating she could not find suitable lodgings for herself and son, but thanking the Managers for giving her a chance. They responded by taking a vote not to employ any more young married women.[29] When Miss Bertha Tuck, the Head of the Infants since 1898, married Mr Ladle in June 5, 1922, she continued in her post for another five years; as she was fifty-five years old at the time of her marriage there was little likelihood of her applying for maternity leave. In place of Mrs Seal a Miss Cooper from Dunham came as a supply teacher for a short time, while John Yallop, aged sixteen, of Bailey Street also offered his services, writing in perfect copperplate, but he was considered to be too young.

Then, following an edict from the Norfolk Education Committee in April 1924 stating women teachers should resign on marriage, when their re-appointment could be considered, but that no women already married should be engaged, the Managers again considered dispensing with Mrs Boddy; it could cause no hardship, they said, as she had children at home and her husband conducted a successful business in the village. Mrs Boddy was away for long periods in 1924, prior to and after a major operation, probably a hysterectomy – her prolonged absence was felt to put too much pressure on the other teachers, especially the Head who, without her, had to teach 93 children instead of his usual 35. Though Mrs Boddy was thirty-nine, and only two years short of a paid pension, the Managers disregarded this fact and while acknowledging it seemed unfair, they agreed to ask for her resignation. But she survived and continued teaching at the school for a further twenty-five years before finally retiring on December 23, 1949.[30]

The turnover of teachers made work for the Managers, not only in assessing the potential of the applicants, they also had to find them lodgings. Miss Letitia Goodman lodged with Mrs Taylor at the Mill House; after her departure in 1922 her place in the school and her lodgings were taken by Miss Edith Juler from Middlesborough. Miss Juler had said that she had friends in Castle Acre and relations in Swaffham. Others who came from afar also claimed local connections. Miss Winifrede Blamire from Staffordshire had an aunt in Little Dunham, whose address was the School House. When Miss Rosalie Clare came from Rugby to be Head of Infants in 1927, she had previously taught at Newcastle, Durham, Much Hadham, Herts, and more recently at Wisbech. Nearer to home, teachers came from Norwich, Dereham and Litcham. A few, like Miss Alice Spencer, had always lived in Castle Acre as had Miss Constance Edwards who lived at Lodge Farm and whom Everington had known 'since birth'.

The resignation of Mrs Ladle, née Miss Bertha Tuck, as Head of Infants in 1927 and the appointment of Miss Rosalie Clare in her place caused one of the Managers, Mr Keith of the Wicken, to write to the vicar the Revd Bek, saying he was: 'surprised to hear of a new teacher appointed to succeed Mrs Ladle – I would have made a special journey from Scotland had I known...' He had a particular dislike of local teachers and regarded the appointment as 'wholly irregular'. Miss Clare may have been born in Norfolk but could hardly be described as having only local experience. She was not popular with the Revd Bek either for when she married Mr Upton three years later the marriage took place in King's Lynn not Castle Acre.[31]

In January 1929 the Head Mr Ruscoe resigned. He had been in the post for thirty-four years and taught in Norfolk Schools for thirty-eight, beginning as a Pupil Teacher at Great Massingham. Since 1926, when his wife became unwell, he felt he had been unable to give as much of his time to the school as he would have wished. This had culminated in an unsatisfactory report from the H.M.I., who, by the purest bad luck, had chosen Valentine's Day to visit Castle Acre; a day when many of the children were absent visiting shops and the large houses. The Inspector was not impressed. He went on to criticise Ruscoe for having 'deviated a little from the approved time table and did not like to see the children bringing their meals into school and not having table cloths, plates etc.' As Ruscoe ruefully recorded no Inspector had ever visited on Valentine's Day before.[32]

After Ruscoe retired there was a temporary Head, a woman, for several months, but by the end of this period, November 1929, some concern was felt by the Managers that the three women Certificated Assistant Teachers, all living in Castle Acre, had 'got somewhat deep in a rut'. It was anticipated that the new Head might have problems with them. Perhaps this was why, February 10, 1933 the Managers decided they would not consider any local person for the vacant post of Certificated Teacher.

The next Head was to be Mr Crowther, an applicant much championed by the vicar. Crowther was known to be keen on sports and Bek the vicar being an 'old Scout Commissioner myself' found this admirable, plus Crowther was a Yorkshire man which for some reason Bek also approved of. However, before taking up the Headship Crowther made it clear that he was not prepared to live in the small cottage that had been home to the Ruscoes.

Over the years since 1839, the Headmasters had lived in a variety of different houses, there had never been an on-site school house, so that providing accommodation for the Head was often a difficulty. It had been suggested in 1909 that the three cottages to the west of the school might be joined to form one master's house, but this was rejected as there was 'no room at the back.'[33] Leaman had lived on Stocks Green near the church gate and Ruscoe in a cottage rented by the Managers from the Holkham Estate for £7.10s.0d. per annum; for which they charged Ruscoe £8.10s.0d. per annum. In the Holkham rent books this cottage is referred to as no. 73 Castle Acre; it had been built in the 1870s by the then Holkham clerk of the works, Thomas Banner, for one of his sons and he named it Oak Cottage east, being one of a pair of cottages on the Newton Road, still there today. Crowther only accepted the Headship on condition he was offered a better house, though he did at first rent Oak Cottage.

Bek wrote that Lord Leicester had promised to give a piece of land on which the Managers would build a schoolmaster's house, but although they toyed with this idea, they could not afford to build. Bek's letters to the Norfolk Education Committee on the subject of appointing a new Head are surprisingly frank and make use of current slang. He stated in January 1930 that Crowther aged thirty-five was keen to come to Castle Acre and was sorely needed. His argument was that with a headmaster of this calibre, the village would attract a better class of tradesmen and 'we must be able to offer their children education on the spot'. Bek continued that the 'School Master of today is better off than the Parson, Ruscoe gets more money than I do, an indifferent School Master would jump at Castle

Acre with its nice fat screw...we do not want a man here to study his own advancement and rush off when he can find a better hole... the Education Committee has Castle Acre on its black list – this man will take it off... he is willing to take temporary accommodation ...' and so on, in much the same vein, and in vain. Despite flattering the Education Committee by saying they knew the history of 'Education in Castle Acre' better than he did and wanting it to return to 'the renowned Educational Centre it was in the past', they would not pay towards building a schoolmaster's house. There was no persuading them. [34] Other suggestions were made, either to rent, or if necessary buy a bungalow that was up for sale (December 14, 1929) or ask the Rural District Council to build a council house for them to rent. (January 1, 1930).

By November 10, 1930 Crowther *was* renting – a newly built council house in Town Lane – but this was not altogether satisfactory, as there was only one well for four houses. Crowther's successor, S.H. Fisher, may also have rented this house. On September 25, 1949, when the Managers were about to appoint another new Head, they were desperately looking for a house for him. They hoped they might be offered the former police house, as a new one had been built.[35] The Head they appointed on September 17, 1949, R.S. Bird, was willing to go into lodgings for a time and six months later, March 7, 1950, he was still without a house. The Holkham Estate would not let the old police house to the Managers and the L.E.A. would not buy the house called Hill Scot for them; they were still trying for a council house on Foxes Meadow and they eventually secured one ten days later. The Managers of many country schools offered a rent-free house, occasionally furnished, to the Head Teacher and the fact that Castle Acre Managers could not do this must have made it more difficult for them to find Head Teachers.

Salaries increased in 1905; the Head was paid £60 per annum, two Certificated Teachers £57.10s.0d., and £52.10s.0d. respectively, and an uncertificated woman teacher £25 per annum. From 1920 teachers were paid on the Burnham scale. In 1922 there were only three adult teachers for 160 children; usually there were four or five adult teachers, but most were unqualified. The school obtained a clerical assistant to relieve staff of some of the increasing paperwork, said to occupy each teacher half an hour on every school day.

Attendance improved somewhat in the twentieth century. On December 19, 1913, 58 pupils out of 143 (including infants) received Attendance

Prizes given by the Norfolk Education Committee. The average attendance at this date was 80%. From 1902 onwards a few children are recorded as winning scholarships to Grammar Schools, but most stayed at Castle Acre for all their school life. Nevertheless the curriculum was expanding. In December 1915 the Infant Mistress recorded a normal time-table:

Morning School was from 9 a.m. to 12 noon with two breaks of ten minutes each and one of five minutes; Afternoon School 1p.m. – 3p.m. with one break of fifteen minutes, with the time divided as follows:

Religious Instruction	30 minutes	
Reading	50 minutes	2 sessions
Writing	25 minutes	1 session
Speech	30 minutes	2 sessions
Number	20 minutes	1 session
Singing	30 minutes	2 sessions
Drawing	15 minutes	1 session
Repetition	10 minutes	2 sessions
Movement: various kinds	40 minutes	2 sessions
Registration	10 minutes	
Recreation	40 minutes	

As shown above, two periods of Movement were allocated each day, during which classroom games were played with titles such as Nine in All, Eyes and no Eyes, Who is Missing? and Hide and Seek. In the playground they played cricket, Kick and Run, Hand Tennis, and Dodge Ball among twelve other games listed; other recommended activities were Leap Frog, Fox and Geese, Last Couple Run, Weak Horses, just a sample from a list of twenty-four suggestions.[36] Half holidays were given from time to time, there was always one on Ascension Day, following the church service, and when the schoolroom was needed for other uses such as a Polling Station at times of elections, both local and national. Sometimes half holidays were given with no explanation, for example on June 15, 1921, when the children took part in a fancy dress procession along Stocks Green.

We know from other comments that the older children learnt to sew and knit and all pupils went for a half hour nature walk on Friday afternoons, weather permitting. A dolls' house with furniture was given to the Babies Class by a former Pupil Teacher in 1909.

Girls and Boys in Fancy Dress, 1921

58

Violin and recorder class 1933

The school had a harmonium from at least 1894 and a piano shortly afterwards, these were played by a teacher to accompany the children singing. Some of the older boys sang in the choir at church services. By 1930 it was thought that the children should play instruments as well as singing and in 1934 the Head taught some seniors how to make and play pipes. In 1935 the H.M.I. suggested percussion instruments for the juniors and there is mention of a 'violin class' (six children) in 1933. Folk dancing for the older girls was recommended by a Mr Reynish when Crowther sought his advice in early 1930 and was subsequently taken up, the girls gave several dance displays on public occasions. By 1940 the girls had a choir of their own, twenty-three strong, and took part in the King's Lynn Festival. Mr Reynish had recommended gardening and games for the boys.

A reading scheme commenced January 14, 1908, with a box of books arriving from the Norfolk County Library. Under the same system as a circulating library, boxes of books travelled from school to school every six months in strict rotation; Castle Acre always received boxes from Gaywood and sent theirs on by rail to Pott Row, Grimston. The library was not a success at first; the Head wrote in November 1908 that it was 'badly patronized'. Books which had been damaged had to be paid for; he records sending seven pence worth of stamps to N.E.C. Often books went missing, and on occasion the boxes either did not arrive or were sent to the wrong destinations. By 1938 boxes had been replaced by a travelling library van and the H.M.I. report of the following year noted, approvingly,

Country dancing, 1933.
Top: Old Mole. Below: Country Gardens

the increase of literature and drama teaching at the school. Gradually teachers began to specialise in particular subjects; in the staff list for March 1933, Mrs Boddy taught nature study, the Head music and geography, and one of the two assistants history.

The Friday afternoon nature walks, which had resulted from 1932 in several pupils, mainly girls, entering essays for national Bird and Tree competitions, led to more outdoor activities being introduced. Encouraged by Crowther and the vicar, a team of boys and another of girls took part in athletic competitions and displays in the summers of 1934–37. By the beginning of January 1932 Crowther obtained the use of a meadow belonging to one of the Managers as a playing field; he owned a camera and kept a photographic record of the school teams and their trophies. It is interesting to note that in these photographs the girls wear uniforms of tunics and blouses just as they would have done if they had been in a private or grammar school. April 11, 1934 Crowther noted that the Boys' football team had won the Rudham District Schools cup and that the Girls' netball team had reached the final. February 28, 1935 he recorded that the Docking School football team had been given tea after the game, a tea prepared by Mrs Boddy and the senior girls. In 1937 jumble sales were held to raise money for games equipment and clothing and the school teams were divided into houses: Leicester, de Warenne, Fitzalan and Windsor. In the 1950s the L.E.A. provided plimsolls and P.T. clothing.

On the domestic front, from November 1913 some senior girls attended short courses on cookery held in the Oddfellows Hall (in the village) taught by a Miss Sainsbury. Prizes for cookery were recorded in 1919. From 1915 laundry classes were taught in the school classroom, though quite how this was done without running water is unclear; nevertheless they were 'conducted by Miss E. E. Robb County Council Instructress'. Laundry work was also rewarded with prizes, presented by Mr Highe, one of the Managers. From the 1920s senior girls were taken in Mr Eagle's coach to the Domestic Science Centre in Swaffham where both cookery and laundry classes were given. When electricity came to Castle Acre in 1936 the East Anglian Company gave a demonstration on Stocks Green of how an electric oven and an electric washer would work – Mrs Boddy took the senior girls to marvel at it. By 1931 they were also taught to make garments which they could wear themselves and learnt how to cut out and make patterns for these. They also knitted. These skills were intended to make them useful in the home and also qualified them for work as domestic servants.

The boys were taught gardening – a school garden, already described, was created in 1932 by clearing the site of a derelict cottage at Pales Green, but three years later the H.M.I. said this was not big enough and work began on a additional school garden, a twenty-two-rod site in Taylor's Pightle. Potatoes and other vegetables were grown. In 1924 boys were learning woodwork in Swaffham and in May 1929 some went to a handicraft course also in Swaffham. In Crowther's time, the 1930s, the boys did woodwork at school to a high standard.

Boy's craft work 1932

Bees were being kept by 1937, the hive and the bees being supplied by the L.E.A. The bees produced about 80lbs of honey in November 1937. In May 1938 the Head (Crowther) was awarded an advanced certificate in beekeeping by Norfolk County Council.

As time went on, the children went outside the school buildings more often. In 1909 they had celebrated Empire Day by singing on the Green and after 1918 they went to the War Memorial to lay flowers and wreaths for Armistice Day. On May 6, 1935 they took part in the Silver Jubilee Celebrations of George V. There were games on the water meadows in the afternoon, by kind permission of Mr Everington, followed by a Children's Tea organized by Crowther, the Headmaster. After the Children's Tea there was one for the Old People in the Oddfellows Hall organised by Mr

Boys' football and Girls' netball teams, 1934

R. R. Ruscoe, who, now retired, was living in a cottage in Back Lane which he had purchased in 1921. Two years later, on Coronation Day, May 12, 1937, the children once again assembled with the village

Presentation of Coronation mugs by the Vicar's mother, Mrs Waterworth, May 12, 1937

societies on St James's Green and proceeded to the church for a Service of Commemoration and thanksgiving. Afterwards they crossed the road to vicarage lawn where Mrs Waterworth, the vicar's mother, presented each child with a Coronation mug. Then those who wished to hear the broadcast of the Coronation ceremony were invited to do so in the school, 'listening in' to the wireless the Managers had purchased the previous year. After lunch it rained, but a fine tea was laid on in the school, followed by games and distribution of nuts and sweets. The senior girls ended the celebrations with a display of folk dancing.

Though the school had been closed for a day in July 1886, to allow the teachers to visit the Royal Show at Norwich, the first organised school outing with pupils was not until October 1926, when the senior pupils went to the 'Picture House' at Swaffham to see two films, 'Our Navy' and 'Dangerous Waters'. In 1935 four senior girls cycled to Swaffham cinema to see 'Little Women' and in 1937 a party went to 'White Angel', the story of Florence Nightingale. In October 1930 some children were taken to Castle Acre Priory, for a drawing class. The senior classes went to the

Day out at Castle Acre Priory, 1930

65

Visit to Great Yarmouth, October 1933

Priory to learn its history and were instructed by the custodian Mr Savage, later they made notes on what they had learnt. The presence of chairs on these occasions suggests it was a day's outing. They were soon going further a-field, to Norwich Castle and Yarmouth on October 25, 1933, where they were taken on a tour of the herring industry, going along the quay to watch the girls gutting the fish and being helped in and out of the boats, enough to make modern Health and Safety officers have a nervous breakdown. On these outings most girls wore hats with striped bands and the boys had caps with a badge. Crowther clearly had ambitions for his pupils, assuring them they were as good as any others, though uniforms were also useful for purposes of identification on outings. On Saturday, September 18, 1937, eighteen pupils joined a school trip organised by the L.N.E.R. (London Northern Eastern Railway) to London. This excursion claimed to have taken in the Tower of London, St Paul's Cathedral, the Houses of Parliament, the Zoo and Hampton Court Palace. In 1942 there was a film show at the school, another trip to London in 1948 and one to Scolt Head in 1949. As far as we know the pupils all survived unscathed. Before the Norfolk Show settled in its permanent site, the showground near Norwich, it came to Narford in 1953, when four senior girls from the school gave a cookery demonstration over two days demonstrating cookery as practised at the Domestic Science Centre at Swaffham.

Girls' domestic science at the Norfolk Show, Narford, in 1953

Mr Crowther and his staff in 1935
Mrs Boddy, Miss Gaze, Mr Barford, Miss Crane and Miss A. Spencer

After 1902 there was a gradual increase in health care provision and awareness of hygiene, culminating in lessons in the subject in 1931. Meanwhile children were occasionally sent home to wash. On February 26, 1907, a dirty and neglected senior boy was sent home because the parents of other pupils objected. The N.S.P.C.C. took up this case. In 1917 a girl was sent home because she was verminous. Medical inspections were made compulsory in 1907, one is mentioned in 1909, but these were suspended during World War I and resumed only in January 1920. However they became increasingly thorough, so that by 1954 they extended over eight days. In 1934 the examining doctor said the children were improving in health and physique, but in April 1940 he was complaining of poor posture and chest development and flat feet. March 14, 1942 ten pupils attended a mass radiography unit in East Dereham. There are records of children in the school being immunised for an increasing range of complaints from 1941.

The school nurse was visiting by 1915; she examined the childrens' heads for nits, supplied food supplements like Virol and iron and visited absentees. The school dentist with his van is mentioned from 1920 onwards, and in July 1922 an eye clinic was held in the school. School milk was provided from January 23, 1935, and was 'popular' by March

1935, the intake increased from 70 to 130 bottles a day, at a cost to the pupils of a halfpenny a day. Periodically the milk was tested for TB; it was supplied from the Wicken and in winter often arrived frozen. When this happened the bottles were placed in a semi-circle around the fender until 11 o'clock by which time it had thawed enough to be drunk. The photograph on page 6 shows children with their milk on the first day they received it.

Keeping the school clean and warm also contributed to the health of the pupils and staff. A school cleaner had been engaged as early as March 1882 at two shillings and nine pence a week. It was difficult to clean the school in winter, for after the children went home it was dark and the building was lit only by oil lamps. School hours began at 9 a.m., the teachers arriving earlier, and there were many complaints that the rooms had not been dusted and fires only just lit when morning school was opened. January 6, 1913: when the fires had not burnt up and the temperature in the Senior School was only 42°Fahrenheit (5° Centigrade) the Head (Ruscoe) sent for one of the Managers, but this did not help much. When the schoolroom was used for concerts the children were sent home early to allow a thorough cleaning of the premises, but after some events the rooms were left untidy.

By May 1944 the cleaner was paid £45.10s.0d. per annum, plus a bonus of £4.10s.0d. for a thousand hours work.

World War I

The school was directly affected by the First World War. To begin with, the Attendance Officer was called up and not replaced. Medical Inspections were discontinued as the doctors were engaged in war work and teachers left to serve in the forces. As described above, Mr Lane, the Assistant Master, joined the R.F.C. in November 1915; he returned at the end of the war but only for a brief stint from February 17 to April 30, 1919 and then left for a post at Horsham St Faith's. There were continuing problems with not enough staff. In April 1915 one of the Managers visited the school to show the children a piece of the Zeppelin 'which did so much damage by bombs in West Norfolk'. April 10, 1916 it was rumoured that poisoned sweets were being dropped from Zeppelins; the children were warned. July 21, 1916, several children ran off in the dinner hour to see an aeroplane which had come down. Some of them did not return to school that day.

The pupils were encouraged to contribute towards the war effort; by November 1914 the girls had already made a quantity of blankets, socks

69

and woollen belts for soldiers and received a letter of thanks from the Queen's Lady in Waiting. In July 1915, a hundred and thirty-eight eggs collected by the children for wounded soldiers were despatched to Harrods. In April 1915 the children collected £1.17s.0½d. for the National Sailors' Society.

Attendance rules were relaxed to allow the older boys to work on the land, for example in March 1916, 'John Smith has permission to be absent if employed in agriculture'. July 29, 1918, two boys aged twelve were allowed temporary exemption from school attendance to go to work; they had reached Standard V. Twice in September 1919 the school closed early so children could gather blackberries.

Officers of the South Nottinghamshire Hussars visited the school on September 22, 1915. December 9, 1915 the school closed at 2.35.p.m. so that children could attend a military funeral.

Armistice Day was observed from November 1918 onwards and the children had a half-holiday when the war memorial was unveiled on June 29, 1921. Many of the men whose names were on it had attended the school and some were the fathers of current pupils.[37]

World War II

Once more wartime conditions made an impact on the school and children. This time the pupils were without a permanent Head Teacher for the duration. S.H. Fisher took over as Head on February 24, 1939, but joined the R.A.F. less than six months later as a Met. Officer at Mildenhall and did not return until December 1945. In between, there was a series of temporary Heads; even after Fisher returned he stayed less than a year, leaving for a post on the staff of Coventry Emergency Teacher Training College in November 1946. He did not return. The school continued to be run by temporary Heads until November 1, 1949. This was, in part, owing to the difficulty of finding and housing teachers after the war. Here, as elsewhere, there were staffing difficulties during World War II. On October 31, 1944, the Managers complained not only about frequent staff changes, but unsuitable staff. A teacher from London, with only kindergarten experience, was put in charge of a class of ten-years-olds. Meanwhile in September 1939 thirty-one evacuees of school age and one teacher arrived in Castle Acre, followed by seven more on October 21, 1940. On July 30, 1944, there were eighteen official evacuees in the village, also several parents who had come here on their own initiative with their children. It was an unsettling time, with no permanent Head and the very real possibility of Castle Acre children themselves being sent for evacuation oversees; in July 1940 a doctor examined several of them with this view in sight. The named ones did not go, however, but remained in the village.

As in the First World War the children were involved in 'doing their bit'. December 1, 1939, they raised £2.10s.0d. for Christmas gifts for old scholars serving in the Forces. February 24, 1940 they collected money for children in Finland. In November 1945, three children received certificates for collecting books and periodicals for the troops.

From March 1940 there were regular inspections of gas masks and gas drill, in which the children, wearing their masks, went through a van filled with tear-gas; the Head records: 'each child spent a few minutes in the gas chamber'. November 1, 1940, all the children spent fifty minutes in the shelter during an air-raid alert. This was an Anderson shelter which had been acquired by Fisher at the outbreak of war and which was used for some years afterwards as a tool-shed. January 29, 1943, arrangements had to be made to black out the school when it was to be used as a polling station, after dark.

Troops were billeted in the school one weekend in June 1941 and that summer senior boys were allowed off school to help with the harvest; in the summer of 1943 senior pupils were allowed to work on the land for a maximum of twenty half-days. In September 1941 the Head took two stone of blackberries, which the children had picked, to the Preserving Centre in Swaffham, where he was paid three pence for each pound, and the money was put towards the Christmas Party. In July 1946 fourteen pupils were allowed to go fruit picking – food was still in short supply after the war.

There were similar problems with coal and petrol. The school had to be closed for two days in January 1942 and for another two days in March as they had run out of coal and the coal merchant had no petrol. Coal was also very short in the winter of 1943/4 but fires were kept going with logs. Demonstrations of wartime economy cooking were given. In 1944 an application was made for 42 pairs of (free) Wellington rubber boots for use by the children who lived at some distance from the school. At the end of war, in 1945, several children entered for a competition by Freebridge Lynn District Council in connection with Thanksgiving Week; entries ranged from toy making to handwriting and seven of them won prizes. That November, poppies were sold in the school.

In 1947 the school leaving age was raised and, with the closure of Westacre School by early 1948, Castle Acre was preparing to increase its numbers; but by April the school still only had five teachers. Mrs D.Elvin, née Ruscoe, once a teacher in the School and now the school secretary, filled in for a few weeks as a supply in 1949. On the appointment of Mr Bird as new Head at the end of that year, Mrs Elvin 'terminated her appointment' as Bird phrased it, both teaching and secretarial, and handed all the account books into his keeping.

Other links with the past were severed. Miss Olive Gaze had died in April 1947 having taught in the school for forty-six years, beginning as a Monitress in 1901 and becoming a Pupil Teacher in 1902. In July 1948 Mrs Boddy, née Bilham, surpassed this record – she had commenced teaching in 1896 at the age of thirteen, fifty-two years previously. A Mr Greenwood visited the school in connection with Mrs Boddy having now reached sixty-five years of age, well past retirement, but she continued for another eighteen months until her 'temporary appointment' terminated December 31, 1949.

6. 1950–2009

Housing for the Head Teacher continued to be a problem; Mr Ivor Pritchard was appointed Head but had to withdraw as he could not find a house. The Managers then appointed Mr Ronald Heaps who was prepared to live in a caravan, but he withdrew a few weeks later when he had accepted a post elsewhere.

Mr Robert Bird was Head Teacher from 1949 until 1974 and lived throughout that time on Foxes Meadow in a council house. During this period several of the other teachers lived out of the village, while teachers who taught at other village or town schools moved in! The log-book entries are very sparse during the 1950s and 60s, when Bird was Head, and give only the barest amount of information. In 1950 he notes a cycle rack was delivered by a British Railways van, two sets of wire storage lockers for plimsolls, complete with padlocks and a potato peeler. He records using a Roneo duplicator but by 1954 wrote little more than the start and end of each term. Bird was known as a strict disciplinarian.

In August 1950 a new vicar arrived in the village, the Revd R.N. Evans who had occasion to write to the National Society and ask their advice on a matter of protocol. Evans was unclear, as the vicar, whether he was a trustee of the School or a Foundation Manager. The legal secretary of the National Society replied that he was not surprised Evans was confused, having looked at the Trust Deed of 1873 himself, he said it was most unusual – in essence the incoming Vicar was an ex officio Foundation Manager and would have to appoint himself! However he was under no obligation to be the chairman of the Managers even if the other Managers would like him to be.

The National Society is still going strong and receives regular school inspection reports.

In 1952 there were 177 children in the school – three years later in March 1955, it was announced that the 26 pupils aged eleven and over would be transferred to Secondary Schools, in either Swaffham or Litcham, leaving 126 children aged five to eleven. Castle Acre became a Primary School. The H.M.I. report of 1957 described the school buildings as five main rooms, one of which was used for assembly and as a dining room, and all of which needed redecorating. The electric light was very poor in two of the rooms and the infants' room was too small for the number of children. Further criticisms were that the pump that supplied drinking water often broke down and that there were only bucket lavatories.

By 1962 there were 90 children on the roll and a staff of three teachers. Central heating was installed in 1963; this had to be done during term time or risk waiting several years for a free slot during the summer holidays. The inconvenience was considered worth it and the work began in November and was finished by December 9. It was presumably at this time that the chimneys were taken down and the fireplaces blocked up.

The number of children on the roll was 96 in 1969, but this fell to 78 two years later. Proposed changes to create Middle Schools in Swaffham were learnt about in January 1972 which would mean that children of eight years plus would leave Castle Acre School to attend them, thus reducing the numbers further still. This duly happened from September 1974. Castle Acre became a First School with just 40 children aged from five to eight. 39 children had left for schools in Swaffham and one to Dereham. Mr Bird, the Head, had resigned the previous April intending to retire in December 1973 but was asked to continue until Easter 1974 as the new Head was unable to start before that date. This was Miss Webber the first permanent woman Head. She was also the first permanent Head not to live in the village, although during the war the temporary Head, Mr Harrold, lived at Westacre and several of the other teachers further afield. In October 1980 she recorded leave of absence for a day for her move from Swaffham to Fakenham. In common with most new Heads Miss Webber initiated several changes; in her first year parents evenings were introduced on June 25 and 26, and some improvements were made to the décor and fabric of the building. Miss Webber was very quick to deal with potential dangers and health risks such as mice in the kitchen. By the end of her first year, in November 1974, a new teaching aid had been introduced in the school involving the use of a screen.

In the nineteenth and in early years of the twentieth century, the children used slates for their written work, writing, maths and drawing. After the 1902 Education Act there was no need to continue with slates, as part of the modernisation and improvements, the Act provided for paper to be supplied by the N.C.C. But old habits die hard and the new batches of slates delivered in the late 1890s were not discarded for some time. Slates were still in use in 1908 when the H.M.I. report recommended they should be withdrawn. Gradually they did become redundant and blots and smudges filled the exercise books as the pupils were encouraged to write neatly in ink. Legible handwriting was both desirable and necessary for the passing of exams and future employment, even after typewriters made their entrance; typewriters were not used in the school except by the Staff.

The very first screens used in the school were for showing educational films and film strips (stills); from the late 1940s over a thousand titles were available from the library at the County Education Office in Norwich, each labelled with recommended age group, duration and whether silent or with sound, colour or black and white. The films were rationed by the N.E.C. to one a fortnight even though some ran for no longer than ten minutes. However, the arrival of the first permanent screen for daily use in the school occurs in 1974 in an entry for Hubbards of Swaffham coming to adjust the set and this was, of course, a television. Schools programmes generally lasted half an hour, and were popular so long as the reception was adequate, which was not always the case. There were many teething problems. In October 1977 a new and more sensitive aerial was put up which enabled the school to receive BBC2. The set itself continued to give trouble and in January 1978, after an engineer from Dereham was unable to repair it, a new one was purchased, but it was still subject to climatic conditions. The following June it was out of order thanks to a storm.

A school photographer paid annual visits from 1974 when Miss Webber noted that he had taken individual photos of the children. A tape recorder was purchased in 1978. The school kitchen was still in use, but after September 1983 meals came from Marham.

During the 1970s Miss Webber made more entries in the log-books than Mr Bird had done in his twenty-five years. In many respects the problems recorded were age-old; one day when the Head was away one of the boys misbehaved. Unluckily for him the vicar happened to call at the school that day and afterwards went to see the boy's parents. The winter weather continued severe and the school was cold; from 1975 the boiler was fuelled by oil, but constantly played up, filling the rooms with fumes. The playgrounds and roads were often treacherous with snow and ice, and in consequence many children who lived more than a mile away stayed at home in bad weather, though by this date they no longer walked to school but were picked up either by taxis or a minibus. One October morning the minibus collided with a car, but no one was hurt. The weather in February 1979 was so bad that none of the teaching staff could reach Castle Acre and the vicar agreed to close the school. That summer the telephone was out of order for two weeks. Thunder storms and flooding caused problems as of old; part of the ceiling fell down in the Infants' room and for some weeks it was propped up with a beam. Only in 1984 was the ceiling artexed and strip lighting installed. Bad colds and influenza, especially in the Infants' class, frequently accounted for low attendance. In 1977 the school was broken into; the police were called, but it was found that nothing had been taken from the classrooms. A month later the school had a half day holiday to celebrate the Queen's Silver Jubilee. A stray dog turned up one January and went into the canteen where it made itself at home and was admired by the staff; the combined efforts of the police and the vicar failed to drive it away – eventually its owner came to claim it. The playground across the lane from the school was grassed over and used for sports days. At Christmas time the children performed concerts for the Happy Circle in the Village Hall.

In May 1983 the Prime Minister Mrs Thatcher visited Castle Acre and the children were taken out of school 'to catch a glimpse of her'. Few outings are recorded in Miss Webber's time, and none outside Norfolk, the furthest was to the Shire Horse centre at West Runton and to Felbrigg. Over these years school numbers gradually fell to the point when in September 1984 there were just 25 children and closure was feared. The Head reported, 'We are working under extremely difficult conditions.' In January 1985 the cold weather was so intense that the oil froze in the boiler and the school had to close. But more positive points were noted: the formation of a P.T.A. and a garden party held in aid of the newly formed Friends of the School when £160 was raised. The numbers of pupils increased to 31. Two women parent-governors were elected in June 1985.

Miss Webber retired at Easter 1986 and Miss Ray was appointed Head in her place, but this appointment lasted only until July when she was obliged to leave for medical reasons; Ms Margaret Cooper of the County Unattached Staff Unit took her place. During her time the first AGM of the Friends of Castle Acre School was held, on November 11 1986, and Ms Cooper introduced a Harvest Assembly in the school, a School Bazaar in December and a School Party with Santa giving out presents at the end of the Christmas term. Ms Cooper's appointment was temporary and in March 1987 interviews were taking place for the next permanent Head. Miss Lynne Kirby was the successful candidate and over the course of the summer term she visited the school to meet the pupils, parents, staff and governors.

Miss Kirby took up her post in September 1987 and under her headship the school prospered: 'the children are excellent and the day went well…. Mrs S. and Mrs R. came in to help with science, messy but fun.' Miss Kirby organised swimming lessons for the pupils (once or twice driven to the pool by her Dad) and a twice weekly Walking Club taking the children along by the river and up through the castle, with impressions recorded later; Mrs Bridgham the Infants' teacher started a lunch time Gym Club and later there was a Wildlife Watchers Club. By 1991 a Gardening Club had been formed and a choir. Applications to be admitted to the school came from many living outside the immediate catchment area and in 1990 they had achieved their quota.

A few weeks into her first term Miss Kirby ordered the school's first computer and she and Mrs Bridgham went on several computer courses, although the computer was not set up and working until January 1988. Pupils got their first lessons on it in 1989; further computers were purchased thanks to a grant, and an Internet link was added in 1998. When the photocopier broke down in September 1991 Miss Kirby prefaced this entry with the word 'Disaster!' How long it had been in use in the school is not known.

In September 1988 the National Curriculum first raised its head and four years later SATS. Both involved training courses, days away from the school. Meanwhile the H.M.I.s were phased out and in 1992 were replaced by Ofsted, the clumsily named Office for Standards in Education, who delivered their first reports in 1994. The actual phrase 'Health and Safety' was also first recorded that year, when a survey was taken; until then safety was largely dealt with by commonsense inside the school premises and awareness outside. There were a number of talks and films on such subjects as Road Safety, Playing near Water safely, and Never go with Strangers. Health had never been neglected, a school Nurse visited frequently to examine the children and to recommend treatment when needed. A continuing problem was nits, or dirty heads as it was referred to earlier. The care of teeth and healthy eating was seen to by Mrs Taylor (dental health education) who gave 'an excellent talk followed by several children giving up sweets!' in 1991. The following day the Walking Club voted not to have the usual sweet en route. But Health and Safety combined needed further study and in 1998 the Head and Miss Jenny Cooper attended a two-day course on the subject. The general increase in paper work placed a heavy burden on the Head especially as the admin days were reduced to one day a week.

One of the greatest concerns about the school building was finally resolved at this time, the building of indoor lavatories. First discussed as a real possibility in 1989, work started on them in January 1992 with the Grand Opening in June.

There was also a continuing need to raise funds for school equipment and activities and the Friends of Castle Acre School were, and are, energetic in their efforts. They held quiz nights, fashion shows, discos, coffee mornings and above all the annual Duck Race, the latter event reported in the *Times Educational Supplement* in September 1991. The school raised money at its annual Fête, Bring and Buys, sponsored walks, raffles, car boot sales and barbeques – and not just for itself but for local charities like Redwings, and international ones, Rumanian orphans, Panda Relief, Red Nose Day and Barnardo's. For some years the children wore a uniform of a red or navy sweatshirt with a white tea-shirt stamped with a logo. In 2001 it was decided by the Head, Mrs Baker, to change to a colour elected by the children; a poll was held and the colour purple was chosen, with an embroidered logo designed by Mrs Matthews one of the Governors.

Guinea pigs were purchased as school pets in early 1990 and lived, and bred, successfully for a number of years. Miss Kirby invited various dogs to the school as part of their Pets Project: police handlers with their dogs, Harry the Field Spaniel with his trainer; a blind woman and her guide dog; a Mrs M. who brought two dogs and explained how show dogs are judged and Honey belonging to Mr and Mrs Joice opened the School Fête in 1988. Other dogs appeared from time to time, uninvited.

The school staff now consisted of two and a half teachers, with part-time helpers, welfare assistants and secretary, besides the caretaker or cleaner in charge, canteen workers and school meals supervisors. Students, very often Castle Acre children, came in for work experience and trainee teachers for longer periods, not unlike the Pupil Teachers of old. Miss Kirby left in April 1999 and since then there have been five different Heads, four of them permanent and one temporary. Mr Kenneth Kay was appointed in 2009.

Middle Schools proved to be relatively short-lived and by 2005 it was decided by the authorities at County Hall that, after all, Secondary Schools were more successful – the consequence of this policy was that Castle Acre reverted to Primary status. With the increase in pupil numbers brought about by this change, there was not to be a return to the cramped conditions of pre-1974, for the L.E.A. announced that a new school would be built on land to the north of the village, not far from the site Thomas Moore Hudson had suggested back in 1870. After many long meetings, delays, changes of design, architects and builders, funding and planning issues, the new school building was ready in December 2009, a hundred and seventy years after the school on Stocks Green first opened.

The change from slates to screens may be seen as a small step, both being impermanent records of work done by the pupils. A click of a mouse or the swipe of a wet rag and all is lost. At present, pencils, pens and paper are still in use, exams continue to be written work, but experiments in Denmark are taking place where pupils use lap-top computers for exams with full access to the Internet, recording their answers onto disks and promising not to cheat. What separates slates from screens are the conditions under which they were and are used, ambient temperatures in the classrooms, less overcrowding and improved pupil-teacher ratios; but attitudes remain elusive, teachers teach for the love of children, for the satisfaction and pleasure of widening their horizons. It was ever thus.

Notes

HA is for Holkham Archives
NRO for Norfolk Record Office

1. HA Castle Acre documents Bundle 11 no. 116.
2. HA E/C1/4 and E/C1/9
3. HA E/C1/10
4. HA E/C1/10
5. HA E/C1/17
6. HA E/C1/ 17 and HA E/C1/18
7. HA E/C1/25
8. Ibid
9. Records of the National Society NS/7/1/2617

10. Ibid
11. Ibid
12. Ibid
13. Ibid
14. HA E/C1/36
15. HA E/S 9-13
16. HA E/C2/7
17. HA E/C2/7 and HA E/S 1-8
18. HA E/C2/7
19. Ibid
20. HA E/S 1-8
21. HA A/100
22. HA E/S 1-8
23. HA E/R/13-30 Cottage rent Books 1901-17
24. HA A/100
25. National Society records NS/7/1/2617
26. Miss Louisa Lurkins was born in Castle Bar, Co. Mayo Ireland but lived in Suffolk from the age of eight or younger; she came to Castle Acre School in 1900 having previously taught at Great Cressingham and at the Girls' School, Southwold. Miss Emma Bertha Tuck was a Londoner; she was born in Lambeth, a very deprived part of London, and grew up there, as had her father before her.
27. Logbooks: in 1915 they paid out ten shillings a day for the Pupil Teachers to go to Dereham.
28. NRO C/ED 68 145
29. Ibid
30. Mrs Lena Boddy was born Emma Bilham in Castle Acre and began her career as a Pupil Teacher in 1896, she was popular with the children and very kind to them; she is described as having infinite patience. To keep order she would threaten to take a badly behaved child to the Headmaster, but invariably returned saying 'Oh dear, his door is closed', and instead wrote the name of the child in a little notebook she always carried, but no more action was taken.
31. NRO C/ED 68 145
32. Ibid
33. HA E/S 1-8
34. NRO C/ED 68 145
35. The old police house, Ivy Cottage in the Newton Road, had been built by Thomas Banner in 1872 for himself and his wife, west of the pair of Oak Cottages.
36. NRO C/ED 68 145
37. At least twenty-seven of those killed in the First World War had attended Castle Acre School, and approximately another six were fathers of pupils.

ABOUT THE AUTHOR

Mary-Anne Garry is a social historian who lives in Castle Acre. She has published articles and given talks on various aspects of life in the eighteenth century from farming to fashion, fox-hunting, food, domestic servants and divorce. She has also published

An Uncommon Tenant: Fitzroy and Holkham
and
Castle Acre – A Social History.